A NARRATIVE

OF THE

SIEGE OF CARLISLE,

IN 1644 AND 1645.

BY ISAAC TULLIE.

NOW FIRST PRINTED FROM A MS. IN THE BRITISH MUSEUM.

TO WHICH ARE ADDED,

A PREFACE; AN HISTORICAL ACCOUNT OF CARLISLE DURING THE CIVIL WAR; AND BIOGRAPHICAL, HISTORICAL, AND EXPLANATORY NOTES:

BY SAMUEL JEFFERSON.

The Naval & Military Press Ltd

Published by

The Naval & Military Press Ltd

Unit 5 Riverside, Brambleside
Bellbrook Industrial Estate
Uckfield, East Sussex
TN22 1QQ England

Tel: +44 (0)1825 749494

www.naval-military-press.com
www.nmarchive.com

In reprinting in facsimile from the original, any imperfections are inevitably reproduced and the quality may fall short of modern type and cartographic standards.

TO

Sir George Musgrave,

OF MUSGRAVE, HARTLEY, AND EDENHALL,

BARONET,

High Sheriff of the County of Cumberland.

Sir,

By your kind permission I am enabled to present to the student of local history another Publication bearing the sanction of your name. To the patriotism of your Ancestor—who held the honorable Offices of Commander-in-chief in Cumberland and Westmorland, Knight of the Shire for Westmorland, and of Governor and Mayor of the city of Carlisle—those counties and this ancient city are deeply indebted; and it is with much pleasure that I avail myself of the honorable privilege of dedicating to his Representative a publication which records the principal events in the history of this city—"little in circuit, but great and memorable for loyalty"—during the troubled period of the Great Rebellion.

By so doing, I believe I render justice to the memory of Mr. Tullie, who, no less than myself, would have felt a proud satisfaction that his Narrative should appear under the sanction of the Descendant and Representative of him, who performed so conspicuous a part as a Loyalist during the Civil War, who lives in the pages of Clarendon, the great historian of that period, and who deserves the grateful esteem and undying veneration of our countrymen in all ages.

I have the honor to be,
SIR,
Your very grateful and most
obedient humble servant,
S. JEFFERSON.

CARLISLE, *December*, 1840.

PREFACE.

The following "Narrative of the Siege of Carlisle" is now first printed, by permission of the Trustees,[*] from a MS. in the British Museum, (Harleian MSS. No. 6798.) To the present period, so far as I have been able to determine, after a careful investigation, no more of this account has appeared before the public, further than a very brief summary of a few of the particulars, which appeared first in Lysons's Magna Britannia, and subsequently in some other publications. Nicolson and Burn, who wrote the first published History of Cumberland, appear to have made no use of it; and the compiler of that History of Cumberland to which he appended Mr. Hutchinson's name, appears to have been ignorant of its existence, devoting only thirteen lines to Carlisle during the Civil Wars.

The siege of Carlisle in 1644—5 forms one of the most interesting episodes in the history of this ancient city, designated by Mr. Tullie, as "little in circuite, but great and memorable for loyalty." I have seen it somewhere remarked, to the honor of Cumberland and Westmorland, that the gentry of those counties, with very few exceptions, were eminently loyal during the troubled time of that which is emphatically called the Great Rebellion.

[*] In the Rules to be observed by visitors to the Reading Room of the British Museum, it is ordered, with reference to the Harleian Collection, that they "will be allowed to take one or more extracts from any printed book or MS.; but no whole or greater part of a MS. is to be transcribed, without a particular leave from the Trustees."

In proof of this, I may refer to the list of the gentry who contributed to the support of the garrison, (pages 39—42,) including as it does, so large a proportion of the ancient families of those counties.

Of Mr. Tullie, the author of the following "Narrative," very few particulars can now be gathered: indeed, the scanty information to be collected at this period, is little more than what is furnished by himself (page 14), from which we learn that it was written in his 18th year; and from a slight notice in Dr. Todd's MS. History of Carlisle, where he is mentioned as "a judicious and observant person, who was in the town during all the siege." From his acquaintance with the classics, it may be inferred, that Mr. Tullie had received a liberal education: he is supposed to have been afterwards in holy orders. His family appears to have been of some consequence in the city, and was settled here in the time of Queen Elizabeth, and, most probably, at a much earlier period. The mayor of Carlisle at the Restoration was named Isaac Tullie. "Mr. Timothy Tullie," who preached the "election sermon," (page xii.) was, very probably, our author's father.

Of the Tullie family, there were three dignitaries of the church who deserve especial notice :—

Thomas Tullie, D.D. principal of Edmund Hall, Oxford, and Dean of Ripon. He was the son of George Tullie, and was born in Carlisle, 22nd July, 1620; after receiving the rudiments of his education in the grammar-school of his native city, and at Barton, in Westmorland, he removed in 1634, to Queen's College, Oxford, of which house he became a fellow. In 1642, he became M.A., and soon after, was appointed master of the grammar-school at Tetbury, in Gloucestershire; but subsequently returned to his college, and became a noted tutor and preacher. In 1657, he was admitted B.D., and in the following year, was appointed principal of Edmund Hall: after the restoration, he was created

D.D., rector of Griggleton, co. Wilts, and chaplain to Charles II. In 1675, he was nominated to the deanery of Ripon, and died in the following year, (January 14th) at Griggleton, and was buried in the chancel of the church there. Dr. Tullie was a principal benefactor to the library of Edmund Hall, and contributed 200*l.* for the repair of the refectory attached to his Hall. Dr. Tullie published several works, including:—"Justificatio sine Operibus," 1662; "Præcipuorum Theologiæ Capitum Enchiridion Didacticum de Cœna Domini," 1665; "Logica Apodictica;" and several controversial works against Dr. Bull and Baxter, on Justification.

George Tullie, M.A., nephew of the preceding, was born in this city, about 1653, and educated at Queen's College, Oxford. He became B.A. in 1674, and M.A. in 1678. On entering into holy orders, he became a prebendary of Ripon, of which place Dr. Thomas Tullie was appointed dean in 1675. Mr. Tullie subsequently became rector of Gateshead, near Newcastle, and sub-dean of York. He died in 1695, aged forty-two. He published a Discourse on the Government of the Thoughts, and several Sermons and Tracts against Popery. He translated part of Plutarch's Morals; the Life of Miltiades, by Cornelius Nepos; and the Life of Julius Cæsar, by Suetonius.

Thomas Tullie, LL.D., Dean of Carlisle, was fellow of Edmund Hall, Oxford, where he took his degree of M.A., in 1678. In 1683, he was promoted to the chancellorship of the diocese of Carlisle, by Bishop Rainbow, to whom he was chaplain; and in the year following, to the third prebendal stall in that cathedral. On the death of Dean Gibbon, he was presented to the deanery, in 1716, which he held for ten years. He died June 16th, 1726, and was interred in the south aisle of the cathedral church of Carlisle, immediately behind the bishop's throne, where several branches of his family are interred. Dr. Tullie was the author of "A Sermon preached at the Funeral of the Right Reverend Father in God, Edward [Rainbow] Lord Bishop of Carlisle," at Dalston, co. Cumberland, April 1st, 1684, which is added to Banks' Life of that prelate.

That copy of Mr. Tullie's Narrative preserved in the British Museum is supposed not to be the original. It is written in the old court-hand, with a great number of contractions, and several blanks. I have added a few words which appear to be necessary for understanding the sense of the author: these are included in brackets, [ ]. On the title-page are the initials, D. B.—probably those of transcriber; and at the conclusion, are the words, *Desiderantur Articuli*. The articles, however, are supplied in the Historical Account of Carlisle during the Civil War, now prefixed to the Narrative.

Mr. Tullie's orthography, like that of many other writers of the seventeenth century, is irregular and uncertain—the same word is variously spelled within the compass of a few lines: this remark is peculiarly applicable to proper names. The punctuation is no less defective, and in many places I have taken the liberty of altering it.

S. J.

CARLISLE, *December*, 1840.

AN HISTORICAL ACCOUNT

OF

Carlisle during the Civil War.*

On the 29th of January, 1638,—exactly ten years and one day before the acting of that awful tragedy, before Whitehall, which made the spectators to give involuntarily one universal groan,—Charles I. published a proclamation commanding all the nobility and gentry of Cumberland, and the other northern counties, excepting those only who were in attendance on his majesty's person, or those who were on his special service, to repair, on or before the 1st of March, with their families and retinue, to their several houses and lands, where they were required to be in readiness, well armed and provided for the defence and safeguard of that part of the kingdom.

In the following year, Carlisle was garrisoned by five hundred soldiers, as there were some threaten-

---

* The principal authorities are—Clarendon, Lysons, Rymer, Rushworth, Dr. Todd, Burton's Life of Sir Philip Musgrave; and the History of Carlisle.

ing commotions in Scotland; but the Earl of Strafford recommended an increase to fifteen hundred.

In June 1640, there being an expectation of the Scottish army entering Cumberland, orders were given to prepare the beacons and to keep a strict watch, and the governor of Carlisle was empowered to use martial law. Sir Nicholas Byron, knight,[*] was appointed to that office, by the following warrant: a document which is valuable on account of the statement it contains of the duties, authority, and salary of the governor.

CHARLES, by the Grace of God, King of England, Scotland, France, and Ireland, Defender of the Faith, &c.

To our trusty and well-beloved Sir NICHOLAS BYRON, *Knight, Greeting*:

Know ye, that We, reposing special trust and confidence in the fidelity, wisdom, and circumspection of you, the said Sir Nicholas Byron, have assigned, constituted, and made, and, by these presents, do assign, constitute, and make, you, the said Sir Nicholas Byron, to be governor of our castle, citadel, and city of Carlisle, in our county of Cumberland, and of our garrison there, and of the works which are or shall be built about or near the said castle, citadel, or city, for the safeguard or defence thereof.

[*] Sir Nicholas Byron was the second son of Sir John Byron, knighted (1579) by Queen Elizabeth. His elder brother was Sir John Byron, who was made one of the knights of the Bath, at the coronation of James I., and was afterwards created Baron Byron: of his sons, who distinguished themselves in the civil wars, four were knighted—Richard, Robert, Philip, and Thomas. Sir Nicholas Byron was a skilful soldier: he distinguished himself in the wars of the Low Countries; at the battle of Edgehill; and as governor of Chester, and Colonel-general of Cheshire and Shropshire. He had issue two sons who both died issueless.

HISTORICAL INTRODUCTION.

To have and to hold the said office to you, the said Sir Nicholas Byron, and to execute the same, by yourself or your sufficient deputy, for and during such time and so long as you, the said Sir Nicholas Byron, shall well behave and demean yourself in the aforesaid office.

And further, for your attendance and execution of the same office, We do assign and grant unto you the said Sir Nicholas Byron, an entertainment and allowance of three pounds of lawful English money by the day, to be paid by the hands of our treasurer or paymaster at Carlisle, for the time being, and in default thereof, out of the receipt of our exchequer, by the hands of our treasurer, or under-treasurer there for the time being, together with all other rights, powers, privileges, profits, and emoluments belonging to that place, as amply as any others have heretofore lawfully had in or for the execution of the same.

And We do further hereby give and grant unto you, the said Sir Nicholas Byron, full power and authority, to govern and command all officers and soldiers whatsoever, now placed, or hereafter to be placed, in the said garrison, castle, citadel, and city of Carlisle, for the safeguard and defence of the same, as well all such officers and soldiers, as shall be and remain in garrison there, as such, as upon any occasion, shall be from time to time sent thither, for the service aforesaid; and that it shall and may be lawful to and for you, the said Sir Nicholas Byron, to require and command the citizens and inhabitants of the said city of Carlisle for the time being, to take up arms for the defence and safety of the said city, and to arm and disarm them as occasion may require, and shall be by you found best for our service.

And We do further give and grant unto you, the said Sir Nicholas Byron, power and authority (if necessity shall require) to use the law called the martial law, according to the law martial, and generally to do and execute all and every other matters and things fit and necessary for the good and safe government of the said city, and which, to the office of a governor of our castle, citadel, and city of Carlisle, doth appertain or belong; nevertheless, our will and pleasure is, that in the performance and execution of this our commission and service, you shall demean yourself, according to such instructions you have already received, and hereafter shall receive, under our sign manual with this our commission, or such others as We shall be pleased to give you at any time hereafter, during this your employment; wherefore, We will and command you, the said Sir Nicholas Byron, governor of our said castle, citadel, and city, that with all diligence you do execute the premises with effect, according to our instructions herewith given you or hereafter to be given you as aforesaid.

And We do hereby, &c.

xii HISTORICAL INTRODUCTION.

When Charles I. advanced with his army to Berwick-upon-Tweed, the Lord Clifford, one of the Lieutenants for the four northern counties, appointed Sir Philip Musgrave, of Edenhall, Bart. colonel of the Cumberland and Westmorland trained band regiment of foot. He was deputed to secure Carlisle, which he performed, and, by the order of the Lord Clifford, left that city to Sir Francis Willoughby, who commanded the Irish regiment.

An old MS. book, belonging to the corporation of Carlisle, contains the following notices of this period:—

The year 1641 Mr. Langhorne being Maior noe accounts were made; In the year 1642 Mr. Stanwix maior; the king made warr ag^t his P'liament, for this cittie was garrisoned by the king's P'tie, Sir Thomas Glenham being governor, to whom was given as an aide and helpe to maintaine the Citty ag^t the Scotch who laid siege against it for one whole yeare, all the citizens plate and money : and in the yeare 1644 the necessities of the soldiers and inhabitants were such, that the eate horse-flesh and linseed-bread frequently; upon which ye Cittie was yielded to the Scotch, and in the year 1645 the visitation begun and continued one whole yeare. In the yeare 1646, the Parlment of England and Scotland agreed for that the cittie should noe more be garrisoned, but p'fidiously the Scotch in the yeare 1648 did enter ye nation and garrison the cittie, but the same yeare was beate fourth with disgrace and this city peaceably surrendered to the parl^t forces Mr. Robt. Collyer being placed maior; upon his entrie the cittie had no money in Common chist nor any plaite or other thinge necessary to be used in the cittie.

The following sums of money were paid by the corporation, for various purposes, or lent to the governor:—

Mr. Timothy Tullie, for preaching an election sermon,	..	..	£1 0 0
1641, for gunpouther	..	12 0 0
do.	..	..	8 0 0

1641, for gunpouther		1 0 0
do.		6 0 0
do.		5 0 0
Lent to the governor		72 0 0
24 Decr, 1640, Lent Sir N. Byron, for paying garrison		100 0 0
for a present to his ma^{le}, which was a cup of goldde duble giltt, &c. cover		28 0 0
the feast to his officers		24 7 0

In 29 Septr. 1644 The counsel of war by warrant required the mayor &c. to raise 300 upon the city—they orderered the moietie of that sum to be raised by free loan.

In October, 1641, the garrison of Carlisle was disbanded, pursuant to a treaty with the Scots; but the ammunition and arms were ordered by parliament to be kept, and well laid up, until the next spring.

In 1644, Charles I. had an army in Cumberland, which, after the battle of Marston Moor, was joined by Prince Rupert.

During this year, the Marquis of Montrose, being pursued out of Scotland by the Earl of Calendar, fled to Carlisle; they had a skirmish in the city, on the 17th of May, and Montrose was compelled to seek shelter in the castle, where he was besieged by the Earl.

After the taking of York, in July following, Sir Thomas Glenham, commander-in-chief for his majesty in the north, came with his forces to Carlisle, where he took the command. The garrison and citizens had taken the precaution to lay in a stock of provisions, (see pp. 39—42) judging, that General Lesley, who had gone to storm Newcastle, would lay siege to Carlisle immediately after its surrender. Such proved to be the case; and, in October, Lesley returned into Cumberland, with part of the Scottish army, and besieged the city. Lord Clarendon observes, that Sir Thomas Glenham defended the place with very remarkable circumstances of courage, industry, and patience.

The frequent removals of the king, says Ruding, obliged him to establish several mints; and the necessities of those who espoused his cause, and were confined to the limits of the castle, which they defended for him, and where they were prevented from receiving supplies from him, were the occasion of many more. Carlisle was one of the places where a mint was established at this period, (see p. 13.)

Ample details of the siege will be found in the following pages by Mr. Tullie. The copy in the British Museum, from which ours is taken, does not give the articles of surrender: these we are enabled to add from other sources.

ARTICLES

Agreed upon between the Right Honourable David Lesley, lieutenant-general of the Scottish cavalry, on the one part; and the Right Honourable Sir Thomas Glenham, knight, commissioner in chief in the four northern counties of Westmorland, Cumberland, Bishoprick,[*] and Northumberland; and Sir Henry Stradling, knight, governor of the castle, city, and citadel of Carlisle, for his Majesty on the other part; touching the delivery of the said city, castle, and citadel of Carlisle, with the forts, towers, cannons, ammunition, and furniture belonging thereto, to the said lieu-

[*] The county of Durham.

HISTORICAL INTRODUCTION. xv

tenant-general, for the use of the king and parliament,* on Saturday next ensuing, at ten of the clock in the forenoon or thereabouts.

1. That Sir Thomas Glenham, knight, commander of those four northern counties, Westmorland, Cumberland, Bishoprick, and Northumberland, (and Sir Henry Stradling, governor of the city, castle, and citadel of Carlisle) with such as do unto them belong, and likewise all officers and soldiers belonging to the train, shall march out of the castle, city, and citadel, with their arms, flying colours, drums beating, matches lighted at both ends, bullets in their mouths, with all their bag and baggage, and twelve charges of powder a piece; and that all such as are willing to march shall have the liberty of this article.

2. That to every member of the foundation of this cathedral now resident, shall be allowed a livelihood out of the church revenues, until the parliament determine it.

3. That no church be defaced.†

---

* 'The king and parliament'—this was the expression used by those who had taken up arms against their king.

† These five words are pregnant with meaning. Not only in Cumberland, but throughout England, so strongly had the leaven of fanaticism worked under the harangues of 'theological empirics,' that "The beauty of the cathedrals and churches was injured to an extent hardly credible; the monuments of the dead were defaced in the iconoclastic fury which then raged; and the havoc made of church ornaments, and destruction of the fine painted glass with which most churches then abounded, may in some degree be estimated from the account given by one Dowsing, a Parliamentary Visitor for demolishing the superstitious pictures and ornaments of churches within the county of Suffolk, who kept a journal, with the particulars of his transactions.‡ This was not enough : our sacred edifices were polluted and profaned in the most irreverent and disgraceful manner; and with the exception of the destruction which took place on the dissolution of the monastic establishments in the previous century, more devastation was occasioned at this time by the party hostile to the

4. That no oath shall by any officer belonging to the Scottish army, be imposed upon any person now resident in the garrison; and in case such an oath be imposed by authority from the parliament or the army, that then any person to whom the benefit of this capitulation belongeth, who shall refuse to take the said oath, shall have free liberty at any time within a month after his refusal to depart with his goods and family, if he pleaseth, with a pass of conduct, unto what place he or they shall think fitting; and shall enjoy the full profits of their estates as formerly, during the time of their absence, and according to the laws of this land.

5. That no officer or soldier be required or inforced to march further than with convenience they may; and that they shall accommodate themselves with free quarters during their march, and a sufficient convoy, to what place the king or either of the king's armies shall happen to be, or to any of the king's garrisons, or which Sir Thomas Glenham shall please to nominate, to maintain them in their quarters, and upon their march, free from all injuries and incivilities that shall any ways be offered unto them; and likewise, that the privileges of this article be offered unto all persons which shall march along with the garrison; and that there be horses to the number of 150, and carriages to the number of 20, provided for the accommodation of the officers, themselves and their bag and baggage.

6. That all troopers as have not by accident lost their horses, may march out with their horses and arms.

7. That no officer, soldier, or any other person, shall in their marches, rendezvous, or quarters, be stopped or plundered upon any pretence whatsoever.

8. That two officers shall be appointed by the lieutenant-general Lesley, the one for accommodating free quarters for officers and soldiers, and the other for providing of horses and carriages for officers and baggage.

9. That no man whatsoever shall entice away any officer or soldier upon their march, on any promise or other ground of preferment.

10. That all such officers, soldiers, and others who are sick and hurt, and cannot now march out of the town, shall have liberty to stay until they be recovered; and they may have liberty to go whither they please, either to any of the king's armies, or to any of his majesty's garrisons wheresoever they

Established Church, than had ever before been committed since the ravages of the ancient Danish invaders."—*Bloxam.*

‡ Recently reprinted (by Parker, Oxford), with Dr. Wells' Duty of Rich Men to contribute to the Building of Churches.

HISTORICAL INTRODUCTION.

be, or to their own houses or estates, where they may rest quietly; and that in the interim, they being sick or hurt, the general lieutenant would receive them, and take care of them.

11. That officers' and soldiers' wives, children, and families, and servants, and all other now in town, may have liberty to go along with their husbands, or to them, if they please to return into their own country, houses or estates, to enjoy them under such contribution as the rest of the country pays; That they have liberty to carry their goods with them, or at any time within a month, and have carriages allowed them for that purpose, paying reasonable rates.

12. That the Earl of Nisdale, the Lord Harris, with their families and followers, shall have free liberty to march out to any of the king's armies, or otherwise to their own houses, or places of abode, at their pleasures; and to take with them, at any time within a month, all such goods as are belonging to them in the castle, citadel, or city of Carlisle.

13. That gentlemen, clergymen, citizens, and soldiers, and every other person within the city, shall, at any time when they please, have free liberty to remove themselves, their goods, and families, and dispose thereof at their pleasure, according to the ancient laws of the land, either to live at their own houses or elsewhere, and to enjoy their goods and estates without molestation, and to have protection for that purpose, so that they may rest quietly at their abodes, and may travel freely and safely about their occasions, having letters of safe conduct, and be furnished with horses and carriages at reasonable rates.

14. That the citizens and inhabitants may enjoy all their privileges as formerly before the beginning of these troubles, and that they may have freedom of trade, both by sea and land, paying such duties and customs as all other towns under the obedience of the king and parliament: And no free quarter shall be put on any within this city, without his free consent: Likewise, that there shall no oath be imposed upon them, or any other now within this garrison, but they shall freely and voluntarily take it, according to the 4th article.

15. That in all charges, the citizens, residents, and inhabitants, shall bear only such part with the country at large, as hath been formerly used in all assessments.

16. That all persons whose dwellings are within the city (although they be now absent), may have the benefit of these articles, as if they were present.

17. That all gentlemen and others, that have goods within the city, and are absent themselves, may have free liberty within a month to carry away and dispose of those goods.

18. That there be no plundering or taking away any man's person, or any part of his estate; and that justice according to

xviii HISTORICAL INTRODUCTION.

the law shall be administered within this city, in all causes by the magistrates, and that they be assisted therein (if need require) by the garrison.

After the surrender of Carlisle, Sir Philip Musgrave, " with many other Northern Gentlemen did march away with Sr Thomas Glenham towards ye King, having a convoy of all those horse under ye command of David Lesley y^t had besieged Carlile. Y^e convoy left them near Worster, and they found ye King at Cardiff in Wales, Sr Henry Fletcher, Sr Thomas Dacres, and most of ye Gentlemen in ye North y^t came along with ye Scotch convoy, did request his Ma^{ty} y^t they might attend him in one troop under ye command of Sr Philip Musgrave, which was granted, and they attended ye King in this way untill in September following, his Ma^{ty} being in Chester, most of his Troops wear broken and scatered at Routenmoore by Co^{ll} Points, Major Generall in Yorkshire for ye Parliament."

In violation of the third article of surrender, "that no church be defaced," they pulled down a large portion of the nave of the cathedral, together with the chapter-house, dormitory, cloisters, prebendal-houses, and part of the deanery.* The ma-

*Bishop Nicolson, in his *English Historical Library*, says, " our sufferings in the days of rapine and rebellion, equalled or exceeded those of any other cathedral of England; ...... our Chapter-house and Treasury had been turned into a magazine for the garrison, and our very charter sold to make a tailor's measures."

In the parish-register of Rockliff, is the following entry,

terials, thus sacrilegiously obtained, were used for
repairing the fortifications, and strengthening the
defences of the city, which had suffered during the
siege. This was a necessary precaution; for at that
disastrous period, when fortified towns so frequently changed masters, they were not likely to remain
in undisturbed possession of the place: but there
may also have been another motive entering into this
act; "the parliamentary officers," says Dr. Todd,
"were so moved with zeal, and somewhat else,
against magnificent churches, that they were design-
ing to pull down the whole cathedral." It still
remains curtailed of its fair proportion, a spectacle
of regret to all who possess any taste for the remains
of antiquity, or are capable of estimating those stu-
pendous efforts of scientific skill, and self-denying
piety, which were concentrated by our ancestors,
in rearing their sacred edifices, while they themselves were contented with an humble dwelling.
The opening at the west end was afterwards closed

which proves the shocking barbarity of the fanatics who were
bound by a solemn treaty to 'deface no church,':—

"Cumberland, Roccliff, at Easter, 1679. John Litle and
Jeff. Urwin being ch-wardens. This register book was bought
at the instigation of Mr. Tho. Stalker, Mr. A. Coll. Reg. Oxon,
curate yn of this ch. of Roecliff, lect[r] of St. Cuthbert's, Carlisle, and minor canon of y[e] cathd[ll] ch. in y[t] citty. There
was not one y[.] before for m-ny yeares, being taken away with
other utenshils of the church, by Scottes armyes, and last
all by Ld Duke Hamiltons, in the year 1648."

e 2

up with a wall, strengthened with huge buttresses; and the space between the wall and the transept fitted up as the parochial church of St. Mary, as the entire nave had previously been.

In October, 1645, Sir John Brown, governor of Carlisle, defeated Lord Digby and Sir Marmaduke Langdale on Carlisle Sands; their small army was dispersed, and themselves obliged to flee to the Isle of Man.

Carlisle remained for some time garrisoned by the Scots, but ere long we find that the parliament grew jealous of them; and in May, 1646, they came to a determination to dispense with their services. Accordingly, they voted them a sum of money, on condition of their evacuating all the English garrisons, and withdrawing their whole army into Scotland. One half of the sum voted for this purpose, was to be paid when the former of these conditions was complied with, and the remainder when they had fulfilled the latter. Notwithstanding this, the Scots did not leave Carlisle until December.

The neighbourhood of Carlisle appears to have been assessed for the support of the parliamentary forces. The following receipt, was, in the year 1794, in the possession of Mr. John Stordy, of Thurstonfield, in the parish of Burgh-upon-Sands:—

I Ferdinand Horne, Regement Quarter-master to Collonel Douglas, Governor of Caerlyll, grants me to have ressaivit fra the inhabitants of Brughe the sowme of aught poundis starling money, and that for the mantenance of the governor's hors monethly, and discharges them of the sumen [summons] preceiding the day and dait heiroff w^m. and sub^t with my hand, att Thurstingfield, the 12th day of Junii, 1646.

Testis by the said inhabitants F. HORNE.
of Brughe.—33s. 3d.

In March, 1647, "there came aboute 70 horsemen with a small number of Foote, to the walls of Carlisle, and having ladders, entered the castle, and broake open the Goale, released the Troopers and other prisoners, wounded the Gaoler and retreated towards Scotland."*

In the same year, the Scottish commissioners, in a private treaty with the king at Hampton Court, required, among other things, that Carlisle and Berwick-upon-Tweed should be put into the hands of the Scots; to this, however, his majesty refused to assent. But no sooner had he reached the Isle of Wight, than the commissioners again repaired to him, and, in that season of despair, prevailed on him to sign the propositions he had before refused. This treaty was signed on the 26th December, and by it the Scots were authorized to possess themselves of Carlisle, Newcastle, Berwick, and several other northern garrisons, with a proviso that when the peace of the kingdom should be settled, they were to remove their forces, and render back those towns and castles.

In the year 1648, Sir Marmaduke Langdale was Colonel-General of the five northern counties; and

* From a curious tract, entitled, "Letter from an Eminent Person in the Northerne Army, relating how a Party of Horse and Foot came to the Walls of Carlisle, &c.," 4to. 1648.

from him Sir Philip Musgrave accepted a commission to be "commander in cheif in Cumberland and Westmoorland, and Governour of Carlile, wch place was seized on in this manner: Sr Philip went to ye borders, and some of his Countrymen came secretly to him, and by his order sixteen men entred Carlile, and presently made y^mselves masters of ye place. Y^e chief persons in this bold enterprize were Mr George Denton, Mr John Eglionby, Mr Oglethorpe, Mr Cape, Mr Wi^{ll} Wilson, and others. This was done ye 29th of April in ye fatall year '48. There was then so great rain and unusuall high floods, as Sr Philip could by no means pass ye rivers until May the first (this he apprehended to be ominous) but at his coming to Carlile many gentlemen of y^t county, and from severall other parts, came spedily thither."

Soon after this, a large body of soldiers, consisting of about three thousand foot and seven hundred horse, which had been raised in Cumberland and Westmorland, under Sir Marmaduke Langdale, had a rendezvous on a heath near Carlisle, and in two days their numbers were increased by five hundred horse, from Yorkshire and the bishopric of Durham. On the 15th of June, General Lambert, who had the command of the parliamentary army in the north, took Penrith, and made that town his head-quarters for about a month. Sir Marmaduke Langdale then retired upon Carlisle, and the citizens dreading another famine, are said, by Rushworth, to have petitioned Sir Philip Musgrave, that his army might not be received within the walls.

In the beginning of July, the Duke of Hamilton arrived at Carlisle; when Sir Philip Musgrave resigned his command, and Sir William Livingston was appointed by the Duke to succeed him in his office. Sir William garrisoned Carlisle with Scots. The forces of the Duke of Hamilton, which, according to Burnet, consisted of four thousand horse and ten thousand foot, were quartered about Carlisle and Wigton, and were now joined by Sir Marmaduke Langdale at Rose castle, whence they marched southward. Sir Philip Musgrave, soon after, returned to Carlisle with his forces; but we learn that the governor, Sir William Livingston, was unwilling to enter into a treaty, binding himself not to deliver up the garrison without the consent of Sir Philip.

On the first of October, pursuant to a treaty which had been previously made, Carlisle was surrendered to Cromwell. A garrison of eight hundred foot, and a regiment of horse, were now left here; but soon afterwards, another regiment of horse was sent to aid them in suppressing the insurrections of the moss-troopers. The county petitioned parliament that this force might not be maintained wholly by them, but that it should be at the cost of the kingdom at large. From this, and other similar petitions presented about the same time, we learn, that Cumberland was in a wretched state of destitution;

many considerable families had barely the necessaries of life, and were scarcely able to procure bread; numbers of the poor died on the highways, and there were thirty thousand families in want of bread, and without the means of purchasing food of any kind. Parliament ordered a collection to be made for their relief, but, from the general nature of the distress, the funds thus raised proved very inadequate.

A large garrison continued to be maintained in Carlisle for a few years. In December, 1650, the governor sent a detachment of one thousand men into Scotland, who reduced some small forts there; and in June, 1651, when a hostile party of Scots approached Carlisle, Major-General Harrison sent two thousand men from that city in pursuit of them.

After the Restoration, Sir Philip Musgrave, who had signalized himself as a zealous royalist during the civil war, and who, in consequence, had been proscribed by the parliament, was rewarded by being appointed governor of Carlisle.

A NARRATIVE

OF THE

SIEGE OF CARLISLE,

1644—5.

Cumberland, a place not seduced with Lecheres, generally free from the seeds of Schisme, and therefore untainted with the psent. rebellion. So Lawson and Barwis found it, when they brought in Sr Arwin* with a party, who settled a committee of strange men amongst them, Craister, Studholme, Cholmley, Langhorne,† &c.; and p'ceeded soe farre as to face Carlisle wth a Rascall rout in 1643. Whereupon, the Gentrie of the Countrie arm'd their next neighbours and Tenants, together wth such as were of the militia, pursued the Rebells towards Abbey-holme, but when they had them in their mercie, dismissed them all upon a sleight p'mise of their future Quiett, which the Roundheads used not to value, without securing the heads of those p'ties: John Barwise,

* *Sir Armin.* Probably Sir William Armyne, who was one of the committee appointed by the houses of parliament to treat with his majesty for a cessation of arms, and, afterwards, one of the commissioners sent into Scotland to desire assistance.

† It is a strange coincidence, that within a few years of this period, there were four mayors of Carlisle, respectively named—Craister, Studholme, Cholmley, and Langhorne.

A

SIEGE OF CARLISLE.

and his sonne,* Michael Studholme, etc. who shortly after p'vailed wth Richard Barwise, a Burgesse in Parl't for Carlisle,† to solicit David Leslie‡ to draw

---

* The Barwises of Langrigg Hall, co. Cumberland, were an ancient and respectable family. Three of them were sheriffs of the county in the reign of Charles I. and the commonwealth. They were anciently possessed of Ireby, Ilekirk, Dearham, and Blencogo. *Arms:*—Argent, a chevron between three boars' heads couped sable, muzzled or.

In the parish church of Wigton is the following epitaph, which it is probable commemorates one of the Barwises here mentioned:

"A memorative epitaph for the worthy and loving Colonel Thomas Barwise, who died the 15th day of December, 1648, ætat. suæ 27.

Stay passenger,—for there bold BARWISE lies,
Whose sancted spirit soars above the skies.
Stout, wise, yet humble, fitted in each part
For more command;—of comely body, pious heart:
Dear to his people, country, kindred dear,
Dear to his known associates every where:—
Who, living, was life's lively portrature,
And dying colonel, lives crowned sure."

† The mayor of Carlisle, in 1648, was named Richard Barwise; Richard *Barwick* was returned to parliament for the city of Carlisle, in the 3rd, 15th, and 16th Charles I.

‡ David Lesley, or Leslie, is sometimes confounded with his kinsman, Alexander Leslie, Earl of Leven. He was an able, though in some instances an unfortunate general, and learned the art of war under the great Gustavus Adolphus. He defeated, but with a much superior army, the broken forces of the heroic Marquis of Montrose. He reduced Cromwell to great straits before the battle of Dunbar, and fought that fatal battle merely in obedience to the pressing importunities of the soldiers. These deluded people were told by their ministers, that they had been wrestling with the Lord all the night in prayer, and were very confident that they had obtained the victory. Cromwell, when he saw them advancing to the engagement, exclaimed, with no less confidence, "that the Lord had delivered them into his hands." Lesley was a second time defeated by Cromwell at the battle of Worcester, where he was taken prisoner, and sent to the Tower. He was, upon the restoration, set at liberty, and created baron of Newark.— *Granger.*

his hors into Cumberland, to subdue the Gentrie and to set beggars on hors-back; this he effected in 1644.

Leslie marched with about 800 hors as farr as Salkeld w^{th}out opposition; but when he came to passe the ford of Eden,which was not very shallow, he found the other side manned wth regiments of hors and foot, wch the Gentrie of Cumberland and Westmorland had raised to oppose him; wch so appalled him, y^{t} he refused to march on, and fell arailing at Barwise, who had perswaded him y^{t} he should meet wth no enemyes. And needs he would retreat to Newcastle, till great Barwise set himself first into the water; and the rest, following him, so frighted ye fresh water countrie whiggs,* y^{t} all of them answered the Motto, *veni, vidi, fugi;* some of the cheif of the Country, whom I will not name, gave occasion to this shamefull flight. †Sr Phil.

---

* "No souldiers, but countrey bumkins, there called Whigs."—*Military Memoirs of the Great Civil War.*

† Sir Philip Musgrave, Bart. of Hartley and Edenhall, son and heir of Sir Richard Musgrave, K.B. created Baronet 1611, was born at Edenhall 21st May, 1607. On the death of his father, which occurred during his infancy, he was committed to the guardianship of his uncle, Philip Lord Wharton. When he had attained his 16th year, he was admitted of Peter-house, Cambridge, and a few years after, of Trinity College, Oxford. He married Julian, youngest daughter of the celebrated Sir Richard Hutton, Knt. Justice of the Court of Common Pleas.

In 1639, when the Scots commenced their rebellion, Sir Philip was appointed colonel of a regiment of foot, for his majesty, Charles I.; and in the following year, he was a representative in parliament for the county of Westmorland, and was again returned in the next year. During the civil war, he attended his majesty at York, and afterwards at Oxford; and he raised at his own expense 600 men, (afterwards increased to 1800), whom he sent to the Marquis of Newcastle; and subsequently an additional 1000, to Prince Rupert at York.

After the fatal battle of Marston-moor, he and Sir Thomas Glenham put themselves into the garrison of Carlisle; Sir

Musgrave, Sr Henrie Bellingham,‡ Sr Henry Fletcher,‖ wth other Gent. would have joyn'd Issue with

Philip leaving his estate at the mercy of the parliamentarians. On the surrender of Carlisle, June, 1645, in defiance of the terms of capitulation, he and John Aglionby, Esq. were thrown into prison, and condemned to lose their lives; but they effected their escape during the night previous to the day appointed for their execution.

Sir Philip went to the king at Cardiff, and soon after, at the request of Sir Henry Fletcher, Bart. and Sir Thomas Dacre, Knt. he raised (as each of them had done) a thousand foot for the service of his prince; but in September, 1645, he was defeated by Pointz at Rowton-moor, near Chester, and being taken prisoner in the engagement, was imprisoned at York.

After his release, Sir Philip received a command from the king to repair to him at Hampton-court. In 1648, he accepted a commission as commander-in-chief in Cumberland and Westmorland, and governor of Carlisle, which city had been seized by the royalists. On the day following that on which the king was put to death, Sir Philip went to France, and remained there six weeks with Sir Marmaduke Langdale; he then waited on Charles II. at the Hague, who afterwards went into Scotland, and Sir Philip was present at the solemnities of the coronation of the expatriated king at Scone.

A short time previous to this, Charles II. had commanded a Writ to be prepared, granting to Sir Philip Musgrave and his heirs, the title and dignity of a Baron, as Baron of Musgrave: the patent however was not taken out by the family. The Writ is published in Burton's Life of Sir Philip.

The Countess of Derby, who is so celebrated for her unparalleled defence of Lathom House against the parliamentarians, gave to Sir Philip the government of the Isle of Man.

In 1655, Sir Philip was imprisoned at Carlisle, his enemies being unwilling to allow liberty to so true a loyalist.

At the restoration, Sir Philip attended his majesty on his entrance into London, "and was received by him with acknowledgements of his sufferings, and promises of reparation:" he was reinstated in some of his former offices in Cumberland and Westmorland, and soon after, was appointed by his majesty to the governorship of Carlisle. Mr. Burton, in his Life of Sir Philip, gives the following pleasing testimony to the worth of his character and the general respect in which he was held:—" when he went to take possession of his Goverment, He was met upon ye way and accompanyed into Carlile, wth allmost ye whole gentry of Cumberland and West-

Leslie, if they had not been   § most of the fugatives took streight for Carlisle, wither Leslie

moorland, ye Dean and Prebands of Carlile, ye Mayor and Aldermen of ye same, wth many others."

About this time he built and endowed the chapel at Soulby, and repaired the church of Edenhall. In 1666, he was elected Mayor of the city of Carlisle, and on his going to London, to attend his parliamentary duties as knight of the shire for Westmorland, he met with an affectionate reception from Dr. Morley, Bishop of Winchester.

Sir Philip's valuable life terminated on the 7th of February, 1677-8, aged 70; he was interred in the chancel of the church of Edenhall, where there is a monument to his memory.—*Burton's " Life of Sir Philip Musgrave, Bart."*

‡ Sir Henry Bellingham, Bart. of Helsington, co. Westmorland, was descended from a younger branch of the ancient family of Bellingham, of Burneside, near Kendal. He was the second son of Sir James Bellingham, (who was knighted at Durham, in 1603, by James I.) by his wife Agnes, daughter of Sir Henry Curwen, knight, of Workington. He was returned knight of the shire for Westmorland in four parliaments. He married Dorothy, daughter of Sir Francis Boynton, knight, of Bramston, co. York, by whom he had issue seven children, of whom three only arrived at years of maturity. The male issue failed during his life-time, and he was succeeded by his next brother, Alan, whose grandson of the same name, sold Levins and other property in Westmorland belonging to the family, to Colonel James Graham, privy-purse to James II., a younger brother to Sir Richard Graham, of Netherby, Bart, afterwards created Viscount Preston.

‖ Sir Henry Fletcher, of Hutton, baronet, was sheriff of the county in the 1st and 18th of Charles I. by whom he was created baronet in 1640. He married Catherine, eldest daughter of Sir George Dalston, of Dalston, baronet, who survived him and subsequently married Thomas Smith, D.D., Dean, and afterwards Bishop of Carlisle. Sir Henry raised a regiment for Charles I. chiefly at his own cost, and was slain in 1645, at the battle of Rowton-heath, near Chester. His widow and family were all sent prisoners to Carlisle, but after a time obtained their release, and his heir was suffered to compound for the estate. Sir Henry was succeeded in his title and estates by his second son, George, who was knight of the shire for Cumberland nearly forty years.

§ In this case, as in others where a similar blank occurs, there is an intentional hiatus in the MS. It appears from the text that Sir Philip Musgrave, Sir Henry Bellingham, Sir pursued them, and drew up his hors w^(th)in view of the Cittye on St Nicholas Hill, neer the gallowes :* a place more proper for them he could not have chosen.

Y^e garrison wth some commons and the scotch horse picquoring [picquetting] a while close by the walls on the east, drew off, after they had failed in snapping Col. Graye's small regement of hors at Stanwick,† with much ado gott into the towne without losse.

Lesly having instantly ordered to raise the coun-

Henry Fletcher, and the principal cavaliers of the county, would have given battle to Lesley, but their followers fled, and disgraced themselves by their "shameful flight."

* Gallow Hill, or Harraby Hill, is an extremely interesting place, not only from its having been the place selected for the execution of the rebels of 1745, but also from its being on the line of the great Roman road from *Luguvallium* to *Voreda*, and from the supposed evidences of its having been used as a place of Roman sepulture. When the road was levelled through this hill, many graves, Roman urns, lamps, jet-rings, lachrymatories, and coins, were found, and also, the head of a statue, the capital of a Corinthian column, and a well-executed sepulchral stone, in good preservation.

Gallow Hill is commemorated by Sir Walter Scott, in The Heart of Mid Lothian, as the scene of the executions in 1746. Until nearly the end of the last century, the remains of the gibbet were to be seen; and at the foot of it, the ashes of the fire used in burning the bodies of those who suffered for high treason. The offenders, it would seem, suffered on the highest part of the hill fronting the south. The hill appears to have been long used as a place of execution; for in a return made to the exchequer in 1610, the bridge over the Petteril is called Gallow Bridge.—*History of Carlisle, and Carlisle Patriot.*

† Stanwix is a village nearly a mile to the north of Carlisle, on the right bank of the Eden which flows between it and the city. It is situated on an eminence commanding an excellent view of the city, and immediately fronting that part of the castle formerly distinguished as the nine gun battery. Stanwix was a station (*Congavata*) on the great Roman Wall which crossed the island from sea to sea; and here, also, numerous antiquities have been found. During the siege of Carlisle, in 1645, a battery was erected near the church of Stanwix, which was converted into a guard-house!

trey for the Perlam't, under ye command of Col. Lawson and Col. Chomly,* marched ye next day towards Newcastle. Y^e corn was then all in ye stook;† and Lesley knew well y^t if he had stayed to beggar the towne, he might have taken it wthin a few weeks; but it was believed, his purpose was to give ye king's perty leisure to victual it, that he and his souldiers might have longer pay.

Y^e garrison plyed their liberty vigorously in fetching in great store of Corn from all the adjacent feilds, besides meat, salt, coles, and cowes, chiefly from about Wigton,‡ ye nest of the Roundheads, in so much that an Oxe might have been bought in their towne for 18^d at this time.‖ Sr Phil. Musgrave was Leivetenant gen^{ll} of Cumberland.

But immured in Carlisle with him were S^r Wm. Daulston,§ Sr Henry Fletcher, Sr Tho.

---

* This is probably he who, in 1648, then holding the rank of major, gave orders for burning Greystoke castle, and Rose castle, the residence of the Bishops of Carlisle.

† Stook is a provincial word for the piles of sheaves of corn called a shock.

‡ Wigton is a market-town, eleven miles south-west from Carlisle.

‖ This gives an air of probability to the surmise contained in the preceding paragraph—that Lesley designedly allowed the city to be victualled and prepared for a long siege.

§ Sir William Dalston, Bart. so created, 16th Charles I., was the son of the excellent Sir George Dalston, knight, of Dalston-hall, co. Cumberland, which Lesley made into his head-quarters during the siege. Both father and son suffered severely for their loyalty. Bishop Jeremy Taylor's " Sermon preached at the Funeral of that worthy knight, Sir George Dalston, of Dalston, in Cumberland, Sep. 28, 1657," may be seen in his works. It contains a beautiful delineation of his character, written in that glowing eloquence by which the pages of Jeremy Taylor are so much distinguished. That eminent prelate states in his sermon, that he had " often visited him," and it is not improbable but that he might preach at such times in the church of Dalston, which is within three miles of Rose castle, the episcopal residence of the Bishops of Carlisle. Sir George Dalston was high-sheriff of the county of Cumberland, in the 16th James I., and represented that

Colonell, with many other militia comanders. S[r] Henry Stradling was Govern[r] of the garrison; and Hudleston,* Philipson Captain of y[e]   But S[r] Thos. Glenham† latly retreated from York fight where he was Governer, was Commander in cheif; and with him came some white coats, and about 200 of reformades,‡ most of them of great prudence and

county in parliament in the 16th Charles I. Sir William, his son, resided chiefly at Heath hall, co. York; where he died January 13, 1683. The baronetcy became extinct in 1765, by the death of Sir George Dalston, great-grandson of the above Sir William, who left issue an infant daughter.

* Ferdinando Hudleston, Esq. of Millum castle, co. Cumberland, married Jane, daughter of Sir Ralph Grey, of Chillingham, in Northumberland, knight, and had issue nine sons, William, John, Ferdinando, Richard, Ralph, Ingleby, Edward, Robert, and Joseph; all of whom were officers in the service of Charles I. William, the eldest, raised a regiment of foot for the king at his own expense, and clothed and paid them the whole war; he was made knight banneret by the king for his said services, but principally for retaking the royal standard at the battle of Edgehill. John was colonel of dragoons. Ferdinando, a major of foot. Richard, lieutenant-colonel of foot, was slain in the minster yard at York. Ralph, a captain of foot. Ingleby, a captain of foot. Edward, a major of foot. Robert, a captain of foot. And Joseph a captain of horse. Ferdinando the father, was knight of the shire for Cumberland in the 21st James I.—*Nicolson and Burn.*

† Sir Thomas Glenham, knight, commissioner in chief of the four northern counties, " was a gentleman of noble extraction, and a fair fortune, though he had much impaired it; he had spent many years in armies beyond the seas." He was appointed governor of York, where he was left by Prince Rupert with too small a garrison to defend the city: within a fortnight he was compelled to deliver it up to the parliamentary forces. He then marched with all his troops to Carlisle, a city " little in circuite, but great and memorable for loyalty," which, says Clarendon, " he afterwards defended with very remarkable circumstances of courage, industry, and patience." After the surrender of Carlisle, he went to the king at Cardiff, with about two hundred foot from the garrison at the former place. In September, 1645, at the command of his majesty, he assumed the government of Oxford, which, in May, 1646, was delivered up to Sir Thomas Fairfax.

‡ When Cromwell and Thomas Lord Fairfax remodelled

pronenesse in arms; as Sibthorp, Woodhall, Colonells Mina, Liuetenant Colonel Maikarty, Macdonnell, Blacke, Wiltshire; Majors Powley, Langton, Rob: Phillipson, Gosnold, Dixon, Marshall, Moore, Birbeik, Bartram, Súibson, Chamber, Musgrave,* Coppham, wth several other Captains; the Lord Aboyne, Lord Maxwell, Lord Harris, S. James Lesley, Sr William Hayes, Mr Barklay, Capt Gordon, Nesbut, wth a few more Scots Lievtenants, Ensignes, quartermaisters, etc. *sans nombre*. Amongst wch Quartermaist^r Wood, and his brother Corporal Wood, Quartermaister Pyr, Hinks, Corp, Vere, Withrop, Scot, John Essans, Rob. Sheild, Brathait, Graves, Laynde, Wilson, Alx. Catcoats, Knogg, Hind, Birdy, were as dareing men as ye kingdome could produce; there were of the Clergy, Mr West,† Mr Tonstal‡ Prebends of Carlisle; Mr Tullie,∥ Mr Goodwine, [Mr.] Featherstonhaugh; Neighbour Ministers from other Countries, Dr Basire,§ Dr Marshall, Mr Norgate; Scots Minis-

the army, after the passing of the self-denying ordinance, the discharged officers acquired the name of *Reformados*.

* Probably Sir Edward Musgrave, of Hayton castle, co. Cumberland, or one of his sons.

† Lewis West, M.A. vicar of Addingham. co. Cumberland, 1636; prebendary of the third stall of the cathedral church of Carlisle, 1637, from which he was ejected by Cromwell's commissioners, during the great rebellion. At the Restoration he was appointed, by mandate from Charles II. archdeacon of Carlisle, when he held the rectory of Great-Salkeld, which has been annexed to the archdeaconry since the fourteenth century. Mr. West died in 1667 or 1668.

‡ Frederick Tunstall, M.A. rector of Caldbeck, co. Cumberland, (collated by Bishop Potter,) and prebendary of the second stall in the cathedral church of Carlisle, 1640, from which offices he was ejected by Cromwell's commissioners. Mr. Tunstall died before the Restoration.

∥ Probably a relation of the writer of this Journal of the siege.

§ Isaac Basire, D.D. (or Isaac Basire de Beaumont) was a native of Rouen, in Normandy. He was born in 1607, and was educated at Rotterdam and Leyden. In May, 1629, he

ters, Mr Thompson, Mr Sandulans, preached by turnes during ye seige.

A month after when Lawson and Cholmley had compleated y^{er} regiments, for the Parliaments servin, Lesly return'd wth his hors and laid close seige to the towne. His works were, one neer Newtowne,* on ye South; another at Stanwick,† on the North,

was admitted into holy orders by Dr. Morton, Bishop of Coventry and Lichfield, and afterwards of Durham, by whom he was appointed chaplain. His Letters of Naturalization were dated the 8th Charles I. In 1636, the degree of B.D. was conferred upon him, in compliance with the king's mandate; and during the same year he was collated to the living of Egglescliff, co. Durham. In 1640, he took his degree of D.D., and in December, 1641, he was sworn chaplain extraordinary to Charles I.

Dr. Basire, in December, 1643, was collated by Bishop Morton to the seventh stall in the cathedral church of Durham; and in the following August, he was appointed Archdeacon of Northumberland. "These appointments, however complimentary to Basire, were merely nominal, the progress of the civil war having placed the duties and the emoluments of such offices alike in abeyance." During this period of anarchy and rebellion, the archdeacon, having been sequestered and plundered, sought safety within the walls of the city of Carlisle, where he remained until the close of the siege. He then repaired to Charles I. at Oxford, and his majesty was pleased to bestow on him the rectory of Stanhope, co. Durham. He afterwards fled to the continent, where he remained until after the Restoration, when he returned to England, and eventually became possessed of the preferments from which he had been so long sequestered. Dr. Basire died at Durham, 12th October, 1676, and was interred at his own request in the cathedral church-yard. Dr. Basire published "Sacriledge arraigned and condemned by St. Paul, Rom. ii. 22," and several works, of which a list may be seen in Wood's Athenæ Oxonienses. Dr. Basire, by his wife Frances, daughter of .... Corbett, co. Salop, had issue four sons and one daughter; Isaac, a barrister-at-law, married the Lady Elizabeth Burton, daughter of Bishop Cosin; Charles, in holy orders, rector of Boldon; John; Peter; and Mary, married Jeremy Nelson, M.A. vicar of Stanwix and Corbridge, and prebendary of the cathedral church of Carlisle.

* Newtown is a village about a mile *west* of Carlisle, and not on the *south*, as stated in the text.

† See page 6, *note*.

this commanded by the Lord Kirkowbry.* Betwixt them the Rivers Caldew run and Eden, scarce passable, but over the Bridges; on the north east were Coll Lawson's work; and Herriby, southeast, near the Gallowes,† belonging to Co⁰ˡˡ Chomley. Yᵉ roundheads wer 4000 hors and foot: yᵉ garrison, wᵗʰ yᵉ townsmen in armes, were about 700. Leslyes half [head] Quarters were at Dalston Hall,‡ not 9 [four] miles distent from yᵉ towne. Whether upon his arivall a party of reformades,∥ wᵗʰ Capᵗ Philipson, marched from yᵉ towne to alarm him. But instead of supprizeing the enemies Quartʳˢ, wᶜʰ they might have done, they made a halt, and stay'd forsooth till Capᵗ Forester came up to them; who with greater numbers, put them to flight, kild Capᵗ Birbeck wᵗʰ diverse others, and had the chase of them for 2 miles. This ominous begining was caused by the jarring of the Reformades, who could not agree upon a Leader nor bethought themselves of a reserve; soe not embodying were easily rooted.

A few days after, Sʳ Tho. Glenham ishued out with a strong p'tie of horse, and a company of Dragownes to attacque Cholmley at Harriby. Capᵗ Marshall entered the work wᵗʰ the Dragownes, but was beat out of it, having received a hurt in his thigh. And this second attempt was successlesse; whether because the horse surrounding close the worke, left no place for the assaulted to escape, or that God was not pleased wᵗʰ the order given the assaylants, in determining not to give no Quarter; but this order was never given afterwards, nor any

* Lord Kirkcudbright, pronounced *Kircoobre*, nearly as spelled in the text.   † See page 6, *note*.
‡ This fine old castellated structure, is situated four miles S.W. of Carlisle, and is the manor-house of Little Dalston. That manor was given soon after the conquest to Robert de Vallibus, who took the name of Dalston, and in a younger branch of that ancient family it continued till the middle of the last century. (See page 7, *note*.) It is now used as a farm-house.   ∥ See pp. 8, 9, *note*.

after undertaking of the Garrison proved uneffectuall.

At this time, command was given to fire and pull down all the suburbs, which begun wth the houses and barnes near Newtowne to Caldewbridge,* which was done without any opposition from the Scots; though the houses were not farr from their works.

A councell of warre being called, to consult whether the Garrison should fight to releive themselves, or expect releif from the King's Forces; it was determined to abide the seige; whereas the succeeding experience of the enemies made it apparent that the 700 in ye towne, wth the Citizens, who all rec^d Arms and p'formed duty, and Co^{ll} Grayes horse, might have given the chase to the beseigers and Liberty; especially considering y^t Lesly had no resolution to adventure his Scots, and many of the country forces were in their harts friends to the towne, and would have revolted to them upon any fair opportunity; hereupon Co^{ll} Gray was dismissed, and marched wth his horse towards the Kings p'ty.

Some 6 weeks past without much action, except the catching now and then of a few Cowes, some Foles acccompanied wth carousing, and some scirmishing wth the Scotch hors wthout order. Forest† was the only man who held the Cavalliers in play, but at length was slain either by Wood or Brathet. His losse was as much lamented wthin the walls as wthout, being the only Enemie of Remarked valour.

But in Christmas, the restlesse spirits, weary of Rest, went out out a pickquering‡ every day, and seldome returned without pray or prisoner. Now was all corne taken from the Citizens, and carried to the Magazeene, a portion thence distributed weekly to every family according to their Number, and their Cattell w^n they were to be killed, taken

* This bridge crosses the Caldew, near the west end of the city, and on the road to Newtown.
† Query, Captain Forester?
‡ Query, Picqueting?

to the Castle, thence from time to time distributed, no more to ye owner, but ye head, heart, and liver; then to any other.

A good while after, an order was published to every Citizen to bring in their plate to be coyned,* which they did chearfully: but this satisfied not the Governors; soe officers were ordered to come sodainly into the houses, as well of Country Gentlemen as of Citizens, and, und^r pretence of searching for plate, to take from them what moneys they found; wch they exactly performed. My Brother twice escaped them so narrowly, y^t I cannot omitt to relate the circumstances:—Once hearing y^t the officers had been wth Sr Thos Wilm. Dalston,† and for his moneys had used him uncivilly, he went to church with a large bagg of money in either pockett; after service, as he was walking with Chancellor Burwell,‡ these searchers met him, and Capt Powley came merily towards him, telling him his poccets sweld to much, but Mins with held him, saying himselfe would search his studdy. Another time, my Mother seeing them come fastly to her house, my brother gave the key of his desk to my sister, bidding her convey the money somewhither; but she had scarce opened the desk till the searcher entred the house; whereupon she was soe amazed, y^t she left the money wth the cover of the desk

* The pieces coined in Carlisle, during the siege, are thus described in Tindal's notes to Rapin:—"THREE-SHILLING PIECE,—C. R. and III. below; *reverse*, OBS. CARL. 1645. CARLISLE SHILLING,—an octagon, has a crown with C. R. XII.; *reverse*, OBS. CARL. 1645. CARLISLE SIXPENCE,—has C. R. crowned; *reverse*, VI.D. CARLISLE GROAT,—octagon; *reverse*, IIII." The three-shilling pieces are very rare. At a sale in London, in 1763, one of the Carlisle siege-pieces sold for £3 3*s*.

† This must be a mistake: it should be Sir William Dalston; see page 7, *note*.

‡ Thomas Burwell, M.A. chancellor of the diocese of Durham, 1631; buried in the church of St. Margaret, Westminster, 25th March, 1673.

open. The searchers demanding ye key of my mother's desk, straitway went to yt room where the aforesaid desk was; wch when they saw open, and by chance covered wth some linnen, one of them laying his hands upon it, said "there's nothing in the I'le warrant, else thou hadst not been open;" soe they departed wth some small moneys of my mother's.

Look not at this short diary to read of Others conquering kingdomes; the plate here in itselfe was inconsiderable. The daily skirmishes were none of them for the defence of the walls, wch the Enimie never assaulted, but aboute ye fetching in of Cattell, or ye tenting (?) ym in their places of pastures, and now and then ye sleighting of a work. More was ye pittie, that such brave men as ye beseiged should be confined to such worthlesse adventures as these, recorded by no abler pen [than] this of a boy not 18 years of age.*

The horse and cattle were now in the feilds, sometimes on one side of the town, sometimes on the other; but not far from the enemies works wheresoever they were. The care of them was willed to 4 Captains, Philipson, Musgrave, Toppam, [and] Scisson; one of wch guarded them every day by course. The horses fed with their sadles, pistols, and bridles with their bits out of their mouths; when any danger appeared, every man put the bit in his horse's mouth, mounted, and drew up for a charge. The Cattell were driven and kept by townsmen.

In the beginning of January, a great body of the beseigers horse, huriing downe to take the Cattell, caused the captain to make wt haste he could wth them towards the walls; but some fresh horse comeing to him from ye Citty, they charged the assaylants, leaving the Cattell at the water side, put them to a hasty retreat, killed and wounded others,

* See the Preface.

took 2, and came in with the Cattell, without any hurt or losse.

About 8 days after, a score of the Garrison's horse, went a vapouring to Haverby,* beyond Cholmley's worke, and were encountred wth a troupe of the enimye, who were chased to their very works, several of them wounded, and one killed; Corporall Rapier one of the G'rrison was shot through the thigh. Shortly after, a p'tie of horse ishued out to Newtowne, the Scots Quarters, who drew out more then twice as many horse, wth a great number of Musketeers; but the beseiged p'ty let them into the town so fast, y^t having killed one, and shlashed many, the Musketeers within the work threw down their arms and run behinde Condall hall,† the beseiged wanting but orders, and a dosen foot to the sleighting of their work.

About this time, Dr. Basire,‡ in his sermon, seasonably reproving the Garrison's excessive drinking, called drifling, prevailed so, that the Governours forthwith appointed a few brewers in every street, to furnish each family sparingly and p'portionablely; for before, such were their hopes of speady releif, and such their manners, y^t fifty bushells of Carlisle measure were spent every week, for tenn weeks together; fewll|| also grew very scarce, which moved the Governours to send out all the horse, (Jan. 4th) wth 60 foot, and all the carts, to Catcoats,§ within a muskett shot of the Scots worke at Newtowne, who brought in the timber of ye houses in spite of Les-

* Harraby.
† Query, Coldale hall, in Newtown; formerly Harrington hall.
‡ See an account of Dr. Basire, page 9, *note*.
|| Fuel.
§ Caldcoats; about half a mile from the city, on the road to Newtown. Edward I. during his last illness, rested one night at the hamlet of Caldcoats, on his route from Carlisle to Scotland, which he lived not to reach, as he died a few days after, at Burgh-upon-Sands, five miles distant.

lye's horse. Half a score of the Garrison's horse went a quarter of a mile from the rest of ye troupe, to a house where they took prisoners four Scots, and brought away two Cattell, and as they were going again to the said house, Captaine Noble with a troupe came betwixt them and the body of the Cavalleeres; but the little p'ty charged him, killed one of his men, unhorsed himself, and brought him away prisoner, without the least hurt, saving one Simond had a little cut in ye head.

At the same [time] six Cavelleeres marching towards New Lathes,* were pursued by Major Barwais and his troupe, and Mr Arnols horse stumbling, he was taken prisoner, and the next day released. The wood being all brought in from under the beseiger's noses within a manner, in opposition, a Musketeere was brought in prisoner with it of Fargesons Company.

The 28th of Jan. two Cavelleeres took two of ye beseigers prisoners, and being pursued by a troupe brought away two hoss and one man, leaving his fellow sore wounded. But I must not omit the out of order, a pleasant adventure, on the 23 of Jan.: Livetenant Frisle lately arrived from France with some Dragownes; All Cupshit came on foot upon ye sands to catch a scab'd horse, but being dissatisfied wth their prize, marched over the stone bridge, wthin a pistol shott of ye walls, and fetched some Linnen from women y^t were there, there being no horse ready at that port, and Frisle playing in defyance of the Musketeeres, who fired at him from the Walls; John Hinks (alias) Read Coate haveing no armour but his sword, Runne towards him and

* New Laithes grange is now a farm-house, about a mile and a half from the city, on the Dalston road. It originally belonged to the prior and convent of St. Mary, Carlisle, and was built by Thomas Elye, the 25th prior: his name, until recently, was to be seen on the walls of the building. It is now the property of the Dean and Chapter of Carlisle.

overtooke him, retired over the bridge unto two horsmen and some foot, where the Livetenant received p'sently from Hinks, two or 3 cuts of the head, and afterwards five more. The Scots from Stanwic sent Livetenant Barkley and another horsman to assist him; but Hinks did so pelt them wth stones, that Barkley drew of sore bruised; but having been twice struck to the ground by Frizle, there came to his aid from the Town, Macarte [and] Swinnow, Captaines, wth Wil. Wood. The Livetenant refusing Quarter, Hinks closed in wth him, disarmed him, and with the rest of his assistance, hailed him into the town by force. Macarte this while killed a Trouper; two more were killed, the lining they got serving for their winding sheits. With the brave Livetenant they brought also a Dragowne prisoner from the affray, wth no lesse then 17 wounds in his head; yet within a few monthes he recovered. The Livetenant was courteously used, and his wounds taken care of, and then released. Sr Tho: Glenham sent for Hinks, gave him a broad

Sr Richard Grame* having a desire to goe to the King was dismissed by Sr Thos. [Glenham]; but he stayd at home till Stakly [Scaleby] Castle was delivered to [the] Scots.† Coronet Philipson was

---

* Sir Richard Graham, Bart., so created by Charles I. in 1625, ancestor of the present Right Hon. Sir J. R. G. Graham, Bart. M.P. of Netherby, purchased the barony of Liddel from the Earl of Cumberland. During the rebellion, he armed in defence of the king, and at the battle of Edgehill, was so seriously wounded that he lay all night on the field amongst the dead. He retired from public life, and returned into the country. Sir Richard died in 1653, and was buried in the parish church of Wath, co. York. By his wife Catherine, daughter of Thomas Musgrave, Esq. of Cumcatch, co. Cumberland, he had, with other issue, Sir George, his successor, and Sir Richard, of Norton Conyers, co. York, Bart.

† This fine old castle—with its shattered walls and encircling moats, its gloomy court and feudal aspect—affords a good example of the ordinary residence of a border-chieftain in former times, when the jealousies and the depredations of the maraud-

therefore sent by Sr Thomas to informe the King of the condition of the Garrison, and ye consequence of ye Citty.

The nineteenth of Jan. the Governour caused 2 cowes to be tethred in ye lands, to invite the Scots to a second adventure: but they had been there before. The same day, some of ye Cavaleres pursued a Trouper to Chomleys work and from thence brought him in.

Feb. 5th; A Numb^r of Gentlemen wthout arms, and Gentlewomen, Rid a hunting into Blockall

ing clans, rendered it necessary to have recourse to every method of defence, in order to compete with the violence of so many foes. It is situated about six miles N.E. of Carlisle, and has been successively in the possession of some of the most influential of the northern families. The manor shortly after the conquest was given to Richard de Tylliol, surnamed the Rider, and from him has passed successively to the families of Colvill, Musgrave, Gilpin, and Stephenson; the heir of the latter, with the assumed name of Standish, is the present proprietor. It is now the residence of Rowland Fawcett, Esq.

In the year 1644, when Carlisle was besieged by General Lesley, Sir Edward Musgrave, of Hayton castle, Baronet, placed this castle in a state of defence, and with his garrison, sustained a siege for a considerable time, against a strong detachment of the general's forces; but was compelled at length to capitulate, in February, 1645.

In 1648, when an army had been raised in Scotland, under the Duke of Hamilton, for the purpose of restoring the power of the fallen monarch, and Sir Thomas Glenham and Sir Philip Musgrave had taken possession of Carlisle by surprise, Scaleby Castle was again garrisoned by Sir Edward Musgrave, as was also his other castle of Hayton. General Lambert, who then commanded the parliamentary army in the north, sent a detachment of his forces to lay siege to Scaleby. The defences of the castle having suffered from the troops of General Lesley three years before, it was not capable of sustaining the attack; and therefore surrendered, after firing only one shot to the besiegers, who are said immediately to have set it on fire. Sir Edward, in consequence of the losses sustained in the war, and the fines imposed upon him after the restoration of peace, was compelled to sell several of his estates; and among others, Scaleby formed part of the price of his devoted attachment to his unfortunate sovereign.—*History of Carlisle.*

feilds,* who were closely pursued by a troupe from Haverby, but escaped. The next day a Cavalere p'ty of Horse went to Commersdale,† from whence ye parliam^t horse drew out, and lined the hedges with foot; but the Cavaleres at ye first charge made ye horse run, and after them ye Musketeres. They unhorsed Capt. Story, Bailife of Brough, wounded him in the head, and [dis] charging a pistol at his back, thought they had killed him; but his arms were pistol proof, and he leaping a hedge, escaped.

The 17th of Feb. a p'ty of Cavaleres took the same way, but meeting wth no opposition, drew home. Hinks, Knaggs, and Arnoll, wth one or two more, staying behinde ye rest, incountred 20 horse, where Arnoll was shot through the arm; ye same bullet rested in Hinks his arme, which kept them long from ye stage of action; at the same time a sort‡ of towns men and women, accompanied wth some soldiers, went to Catcoats to cutt down trees for fuell, all day long, wch they brought away wthout opposition.

Sr Thomas Glenham admireing ye sweet temper of ye Enimie, sayled out himselfe next morning, wth all ye horse and two hundred foot, with scaling ladders and fire balls, he with my Lord Aboyn, Macarte, Philipson, Cap. Surmow, Nesbut, leading ye several divisions; before them were sent out 2

---

* Blackhall, or Blackwell, is a village, within the parish of St. Cuthbert, Carlisle, and about two miles south of the city.—The manor was given by Henry I. to Odard de Logis, Baron of Wigton, from whose descendants it passed to Sir Robert Parving, Lord Chancellor and Lord High Treasurer. It continued in that family a few descents, and then passed by purchase to Sir William Stapleton, who sold it to Lord Dacre. In 1716, the coheiresses of the Earl of Sussex, the representative of the Lords Dacre of the South, sold this manor *inter alia* to Sir Christopher Musgrave, Bart. of Edenhall, ancestor of Sir George Musgrave, Bart. the present lord.

† Cummersdale, a hamlet opposite Blackhall, on the left bank of the Caldew, is within the parish of St. Mary, Carlisle.

‡ Sortie.

or 3 scouts to beat of their scouts, y^t the horse and foot behinde might not be discovered; wch done, the scouts retreated. Whereupon ye Scots sent out 6 or 7 horse to pickere wth the other three scouts, who, espieing the body of the Cavaleres advanced wthin a Muskett shott of their works, galloped back. They in ye work run all away, not staying the fireing of one Muskett; soe instantly the Cavaleres foot sleighted their works, and the horse pursued, but could not reach the enemy; only, in their return, they took ye Commander of the work, Livetenant Kenniby, killed four, and took 24 Muskateres, who had all better Quarter than their unparelled Cowardice deserved. With them were brought of a great Number of cloaks and arms, with the said prisoners, and six Cowes. Lesley, the next morning, raised his worke againe.

Feb. 16, half a score of Scotts Commanders all foxed* came over the water at Etterby† and marched as far as   bridge, where one of them was shott in ye breast, and another had his horse shot under him; whereupon the foxt Scotts made a sober retreat.

The shot horse was fetched into the town; being a very stately beast, very fat, and because he was not to be cured, Sr Thomas Glenham eat him at his own Table. This was the first horse flesh y^t was eaten in Carlisle seige.

This theire bravado was so sudden and unexpected, that very few issued out of ye garrison before they were gone; Cap. Lainyon was one, who makeing haste to the bridge, tooke a horse from a boy, and charged their leader, Capt. Pattin; who, finding himselfe wounded, flied towards New Leathes, which before he could reach, Lanian overtook him, and brought him in, who died the next morning.

* Intoxicated.
† Etterby is a hamlet, in the parish of Stanwix, one mile north-west of Carlisle, on the opposite or right bank of the Eden.

About this time there was a common report that Capt Forester* appeared often at the round head's worke at Botcherby;† fiercely demanding of y^m if they were not yet converted to the King; when they replyed "no," hee was wont to call on Cap. Philipson to fall upon them with horse and foot. Instantly to their Imaginations, horse and foot fired upon them, and they answered them wth shott from the worke, wch being heard at Stanwix, some horse were sent to assist them, two of which were drowned in crossing the ford at Rickerby.‡ Major Barwis, being asked by Philipson at a parley of the truth hereof, protested he could bring 500 souldiers eye witnesses of it.

On the 28th Instant, Philipson and Major Wiltshire rid out wth 16 horse towards   only to take the aire; the Roundheads marched towards them with 60 horse and foot, but durst not engage. From thence they raked towards Botcherby, along ye Riverside, where was drawn out a troupe of horse, and about 40 or 50 foot. By this time, ten Cavaleres came to Philipson, who charging through the foot, killed eight, took 6, and pursued the rest to their workes. Their releif was newly come up, which made the Roundheads horse 180; but seeing the Cavaleres on the backs of their fellows, durst not releive them. The forenamed Hereby* hors made a show of dogging the Cavaleres at their pursuit, but were so galliantly kept in play by three and no more, Knaggs, Corporall Vere, [and] Ja^s

---

* Captain Forester was previously killed, see page 12.

† Botcherby—in these pages variously spelled, Botcherby, Bocharby, and Bocherby—is a village, in the parish of St. Cuthbert, Carlisle, one mile east of the city.

‡ Rickerby is a village, on the north or right bank of the Eden, in the parish of Stanwix, one mile and a half north-east of Carlisle. Rickerby House is the seat of George Head Head, Esq.

* Harraby is variously spelled by Mr. Tullie—Hereby, Haverby, Hoverby, Heryby, &c.

Evins, y^t their 60 horse could not advance 20 yards in a Quarter of an hour; yet these three being above a Quarter of a mile from Philipson, put them all to the Chase, in which Vere being close at their backs was unfortunately shot into the breast, and some 4 dayes after died.

This Allarum being taken at Cummersdale, Blackhall, and Hoverby, drew 200 horse of the Roundheads to St Nicolaus. Our valient
them in their return home, but they sweet soules, came but to show their faces and turn their backs; soe the Cavaleres came in with the losse of one man, but that one worth 40 of theirs.

Upon the 1 of March, Corporall Wood and Livetenant Brathet, went out of ye city unknowne to any, who having killed a Skout about Bocherby, got safe through the country to ye Prince's Army, and Cholmly had a parly, to whom was sent, Col. Woodell, Cap. Gosnold, and Capt Philipson; at the meeting the sack was merrily treated; but about twenty Country Gentlemen, who were brought by Col. Lawson, to see the articles concerning the rendering of the town, wondred that the meeting was broken up, and no such matter intended. Our Provision now decreasing, there was allowed but half a hoop of Corn a week, for every one; though in the Magazine there were 2100 bushells.

March 1. Intelligence was brought in of the Prince's forces about Ferribridge, y^t he had rooted Fairfax, killed 2000, and taken stores of Prisoners, and arms; thereupon, as we were informed, Lesly was about to quit his Quarters, and Philipson was sent out that way to observe his motion, March 12, but the enemie not stirring, Philipson went from thence towards Newlathes, and sent a p'ty before towards Cummersdale, viz: ten horse, who met with a company of foot, of whom they pistol'd 4 or 5. The pikes that day shewed themselves souldier like, by keeping of the horse till the company had reached the Towne, before Philipson could reach with his p'ty.

March 14 about Pontefract.

March 17: The Gallant and faithfull Coronet Philipson returned from soliciting ye King for ye Cittyes releif. In his return, he was taken prisoner at Wetherby, and carried to York. Where Fairfax found the Kings Letter about him, and by the councell of Warr sentenced him to be racked the next morning; but he leaped the walls y^t night, and wth the assistance of Mr. Watson of Corkfeild came safe to Carlile, wth the Kings p'mise to releive them before the ninth day of May; wth newes alsoe [of] the releif of Pontefract, at which he was an actor. Which good newes was entertained with bonefires that night, and discharge of Canons.

2 dayes after, this dareing youth went out with 12 horse towards Blackhall; where, as he was charging a troupe of 60 Horse, he was surrounded wth two other troupes from Bocherby and Heryby; some of which catching his horse by the bridle, offered him quarter, which he scorned to receive, and wounding those y^t were next him, maintained his retreat, without losse of any, only Richard Grave was run into the back by Major Cholmley, but p'sently recovered.

Before they came in at the Port, they were commanded by Sr Thomas Glenham to march to Newtowne. The Scots Quarter, being advanced as far as Catcoats, they saw the enemie, with five times their number, drawing neere them, whom they charg'd with pistoll, and having killed one of their Commanders broke resolutely in amongst [them,] and put them to a retreat. The Cavalleres and their horse being weary, they came in without the least hurt, save a cut in the face of Philipson's horse.

March: 22. The Town had Intelligence, y^t Westmerland men were come to their releife, and

Penrith;* this News the enemie sent in, hoping to have surprized ye Garrison's horse, but they failed of catching old birdes wth Chaffe.

March the 24th, was the last day of 7 weeks in which the Cittye contributed 60 li. p moneth towards the souldiers pay.

March: 26. Capt. Gordon and Capt. Dixon, ranging towards Cummersdale, brought in two Scouts.

March: 28. The pleasantnesse of the day invited Sr Thomas Glenham, wth many other Gent. and Gentlewomen, to take the aire neere Bocherby; agt whom the enemie drawing out all their horse, stood to see them course a Haire and take it, under their noses; some week opposition they made, but Capt. Dixon having run one of them up to the hilts, they fairely drew homewards. That evening Cap. Lanian brought in a trouper from Hoverby. During this time, Quartermaster Wood, Tho: Scot with two more rid towards Bocherby, to whom the couragious Capt. Rose, wth Livet: Johnson, advanced wth their troupes. Rose, wth half a dosen more, marched a great way, before the rest. Wood retreated to the end of a stony lane, who having Rose wth his Mirmidons, inclosed in the same lane, faced about, with none but Scot with him; whereupon the Capt. retreated faster than he advanced; and after he had received as many blows as Wood could give him in riding of 80 yards, he got safe away, by the strength of his armes, with all his troupe to their worke: if the other two had come close up to him, they had taken him prisoner.

March 30th. A skoute was brought in prisoner, from Commersdale. In the afternoon, Quart:† Wood, Knagg, Scot, with two of Sr Tho. Glenhams servants, Rid towards Bocherby, without order, charged through 50 horse, and put them to a retreat.

* Penrith is a market-town, 18 miles south of Carlisle.
† Quartermaster.

SIEGE OF CARLISLE. 25

Wood, comeing of, found himselfe shott between the belly and the thigh, and was hardly p'suaded not to charge them againe, but of this wound he died within a few dayes. The Garrison lost here a man of unparalled courage and judgment in armes; yea they lost more men in such unwarrantable skirmishes without ord⁸, then in all commanded services in y⁵ siege.

April 3. Provision for horse was now exhausted in the Towne, such as but the Thatch of houses offered them; shortly after, they were Guarded to grasse. Sʳ Tho: Glenham, being very desirous to trye what the Country would doe for the Garrisons releife, sent out Sʳ Thoˢ Dakers,* with match and powder to his Tenants, who returned wᵗʰ their p'misset† to fall upon   , the 6th of Aprill. It was intended after the Scotts were beaten out of the worke, to man it, and keep yᵗ quarter open; but at the time appointed, the heart of the Gilslanders‡ failed them, and they durst not come. That morning, all the horse in the Towne were commanded to surprize some Cattell at Scotby. They were drawn into 5 p'ties; every division consisting of about 30 horse. Capt Dixon with his

* Sir Thomas Dacre, of Lanercost, knight, great-grandson of Sir Thomas Dacre, who had a grant of the priory of St. Mary, Lanercost. He married Dorothy, daughter of Sir Thomas Braithwaite, of Warcop, knight. His name appears in the list of contributors towards the support of the garrison of Carlisle, during the civil war. Richard, his younger brother, was created a banneret on tho field, 6th Charles I.

† Promise.

‡ The barony of Gilsland comprises the several manors of Brampton, Farlam, Talkin, Nether Denton, Upper Denton, Irthington, Laversdale, Newby, Askerton, Walton Wood, Troddermain, Hayton, Cumwhitton, Castlecarrock, and Cumrew; and the Out Manors of Lanercost, Brackenthwaite, and Newbiggin, Ainstable, Walby, Crosby-upon-Eden, and Brunstock, in the County of Cumberland; and also the Out Manors of Featherstone and Thirlwall, in the county of Northumberland.

D

thirty, was ordered to ride straight to the place; and to bring away as many cattell as he could. The p'tye, consisting of 42 all reformade officers, were commanded by Livetenant Col Mins, [and were] ordered to stay at the water side, near Hereby, to keep in that work. Y^c 3^d was committed to ye Governours victorious troupe, under Captain Philipson, who was ordered to face Bocherby. The 4th p'ty, consisting of 16 horse, were commanded by Captaine Scisson, who was ordered to advance up to the gallowes hill, to face Harriby not farr from him.

On ye other side, Cap Toppam, wth 12 horse stood at St Nicholas hill, to face them at Hoverby. In the last were 20 Dragownes ordered to maintaine the   at the ford, in case of the forced retreat, which they were seldom troubled with, led by Livetenant   . Dixons p'ty was gone half a mile before the rest marched out of the Towne; he drove homewards 42 Cowes. The roundheads horse began to draw out against him, but were let in by Philipson. Then they sent out a company of Musketeres, to a place called Durham Hill,* by which Dixon of necessity was to bring the Cowes. Philipson was p'vented by a great bog, from falling upon them, but Dixon resolutely drove ye Cattell within 20 yards of them, and with the Losse of one horse, and one Cow, brought them home. Those of Hereby came wth horse and foot, to reskue the Cattell; against whom Mins sent 14 horse, to divert them; but they despising the number, or not mindeing them, marched by them.

Lainan, one of the 14, not used to be sleighted, fell in with the rest upon their flank, rooted horse and foot, and chast y^m through the towne, having slaine 5 or 6, wounded many more, amongst whom was Livetenant Anderson shot in ye thigh, and re-

* Durran-hill, one mile and a half east of Carlisle, near the village of Botcherby.

tired with two prisoners, without any Losse, but a servant of Col. Wodells shot in the belly, who died the next day after.

About this time the governour had sundry desines, but the enimie boasting they had notice of them, one John Head was suspected, who p'tended to fetch vittells out of the Country; but this cheif errand was to betray the Citty. This Head they apprehended, and found about him a Letter from Dick Lowry in the Garrison, writt to his wife at Wigton, wishing her to acquaint Major Barwis, that the towne could not subsist above 3 weeks, &c. Whereupon, Head was committed to ye Marshall Generall, till further order.

Aboute this time, Coronet Philipson adventured to surprise Lawsons Isle, the   whereof, tooke ye sacrament to surrender it to him, but betrayed them; soe y^t he, with divers of the country of his design, Brouham, Mr Musgrave, Mr Denton, [and] James Walker; and came into Carlisle, April 28th. Head confessed his Treason on the Rack; and Lowry alsoe, who was racked wth him.

The next day, the guard of ye cattell was to be commanded by Cap. Toppam, who could not advance to Catcoats bank, by reason of some Musketeres placed in ye old Walls; but with an addition of Horse from the towne, he tooke the hill, and kept it with the Cattell under it. Presently after, Capt. Noble, Livetenant Frizle, Quondam prisonners, with divers other Scotch Commanders, came to Capt. Philipson, being then upon the Hill, and sent for good store of sack, on purpose to fox* the Garrisons Commanders, and soe to gaine the Cattell. And indeed, some of them were so drunk, y^t they could hardly sit on horseback. Capt. Noble secretly employed some to fetch in great numbers of Scotch Horse; who, having got all things ready for his

* Intoxicate.

purpose, drew out in five bodies, about five in the afternoon, each consisting of 50 horse, who fell all upon Philipson, who had onely half a dosen horse with him; but the rest that were grazing under the hill, were p'sently put in order, by Coronett Philipson, his brother; himselfe the while keeping his ground, though continually engaged amongst them. There suddenly began a very hot skirmish, not to be descerned for the smoake, till the Philipsons put ye Scots to a retreat; yet they were handsomely bought of by the Scotch officers in the arreare, who were the greatest part of Lesly his Regiment. The Cavelleres in this Ingagem^t were 80 horse, who p'formed as neat a piece of service as was at any time during the Seige.

April 23. The Cattell grazed on ye other side of ye towne; the enemie made a show of coming down to them, where one * with a servant of Sr Tho. Glenhams, till another shott his horse and him into the hoole. The Roundheads not able to stand before the Cavalleres horse, betook themselves to a piece of pollicie; they suborn'd great Companies out of Westmerland, to come and rendevoze at Penrith, who gave out their intent was to beat the Scots from Carlisle; supposing y^t Sr Thomas Glenham would send out all his horse to head them. He ordered 3 horse on the 22 Instant to ride to Brougham Castle,† who were theire taken prisonners; where as if they had returned with fair promises, they might have surprised all the country commanders in the Garrison, who were resolved to goe forth to conduct them.

* Probably the word omitted here should be 'remained.'

† Brougham castle, in Westmorland, about one mile S. E. of Penrith, was included in the grant of the barony of Westmorland to Robert de Veteriponte, by King John. It has always been held "separate from, and independent of, the manor," in the possession of the noble families of Veteriponte, Clifford, and Tufton. The founder is unknown in history;

SIEGE OF CARLISLE. 29

About this time, the Cowes were near spent, whereupon, April y⁰ 23, all the horse were divided

Mr. Grose supposes the castle to be indubitably Roman; but it appears by an inquisition taken after the death of John de Veteriponte, about the year 1297, during the minority of his son Robert, ward to the prior of St. Mary's, Carlisle, that the "walls and house" of Brougham had been suffered by the said prior, to go to decay; and from the expression 'house,' it has been conjectured that the building was not then castellated.

The above Robert de Veteriponte having been engaged in rebellion against Henry III., and dying of his wounds, his estates were seized; but, at the intercession of Prince Edward, they were restored to his daughters Idonea and Isabella. The elder having died without issue, her moiety fell to the heirs of Isabella, who married Roger de Clifford, son and heir of Roger Clifford of Clifford castle, co. Herts. This is he who built the greatest part of Brougham castle, and placed the following laconic inscription over the door of the inner gate—
This Made Roger. This appears to have been imitated by William of Wykeham, who put over the gates of Windsor castle--*Hoc fecit Wickham.* The order of these words might be derived from the Latin phrase—*Hoc (opus) fecit Rogerus*—placed on ancient buildings.

Roger de Clifford, great-grandson of the above Roger, built great part of the north-east side of the castle fronting the Eamont, where he placed his own arms—Chequy, a fesse, impaling those of his wife, Matilda de Beauchamp, daughter of the Earl of Warwick—A fesse between six cross crosslets.

In the reign of Henry IV. the castle was represented as being in a state of desolation, having been wasted by the Scots.

In the year 1617, this castle was honoured by a royal visit: Francis Earl of Cumberland entertained James I. here, with great splendour, on the 6th, 7th, and 8th of August, on his return from Scotland.

It appears to have been again desolated at no distant period, as it was repaired in 1651 and 1652, by Anne, Countess of Pembroke, who caused this inscription to be put on the wall:—

"This Brougham castle was repaired by the ladie Anne Clifford, countesse dowager of Pembrooke, Dorsett, and Montgomery, baronesse Clifford, Westmerland, and Veseie, ladie of the honour of Skipton in Craven, and high sheriffesse by inheritance of the countie of Westmerland, in the yeares 1651 and 1652, after it had layen ruinous ever since about August 1617, when king James lay in it for a time in his journie out of Scotland towards London, until this time.

into 4 p'ties: the first was commanded by Coronett Philipson and Capt Musgrave; the second by Capt Philipson and Capt Scisson. These 2 p'ties were directed to crosse the ford near Etterby, and to fetch what Cattell they found near Cargo.* The 3^d was commanded by Toppam, who had that day the guard of the Cattell. The last, consisting of reformades, were commanded by Mins, who were to joyne wth Toppam, to face the Scots at Newtowne, and to keepe them in; and with these 2 Captaines were 40 or 45 foot. The 2 first p'ties were fired upon, in the water, from a little work at Etterby; but making no stoppe there, they marched to Cargo wthout further opposition; and brought back from thence 67 Cowes. The Scots at Newtowne seeing the Cowes, made a shoe of comeing down to reskue them; but, alas, they durst not; Mins was in the way. The Cargo people run after ye Caval-

"Isa. Chap. 58. Verse 12.
"God's name be praised."

The Countess, in her MS. Memoirs, says, "After I had been there myself to direct the building of it, did I cause my old decayed castle of Brougham to be repaired, and also the tower called the Roman Tower, in the said old castle, and the court house, for keeping my courts in, with some dozen or fourteen rooms to be built in it upon the old foundation." The tower of leagues, the Pagan tower, and a state room called Greystocke Chamber, are mentioned in her Memoirs; but the room in which her father was born, her "blessed mother" died, and King James lodged in 1617, she never fails to mention, as being that in which she laid, in all her visits to this place. A garrison of foot soldiers was put in it for a short time, in August, 1629. After the death of the Countess it appears to have been neglected. Its stone, timber, and lead, were sold for 100l. to Mr. John Monkhouse and Mr. Adderton, two attornies in Penrith, who disposed of them in public sales, the first of which was on the Coronation of George I. 1714. The wainscotting was purchased by the neighbouring villagers, among whom specimens of it still remain.—*Hodgson's Westmorland, Nicolson and Burn, &c.*

* Cargo is a village, in the parish of Stanwix, about three miles N.W. of Carlisle.

leres, beseeching them to baste the basterly Scots, who had p'mised safety to them and their Cattell: whereupon the Cattell were sent in by 10 Troupers; and the Philipsons marched up to Mins and Toppam upon Catcoats hill. Toppam had ye honour of ye forlorn hopes, and gave them a gallant charge; but received a shott in his belly, of which he shortly died. Capt. Philipson fell on next; who beat them out of ye towne, and pursued them on ye moore. Another p'ty of Scots was charged by little Coronett Philipson, who rooted them with 16 horse, chasing them towards Newlathes, where the Reformades came up, who wounded and took divers Scots.

The foot this while stayed at Newtowne; where meeting with a barrel of strong ale, [they] gave over fireing at the work and Towne; which encouraged the Scotch foot to fire upon them; who shot one through the nose, when the can was at his mouth. After him they hurt another, and killed a third, and were all so drunk y^t when they returned into the towne, they forgot to bring him of. In conclusion, the horse and foot drew of with 16 prisonners of horse, abundance of Cloaks, hatts, horses, and other things, with no losse but what is before mentioned. Toppam was buried the next day, with all Martiall solemnityes p'per to his funerall. The Scots, to prevent such shamefull afterclapps, raised a little work, on the top of Catcoats bank, whereby they secured their own grounds, to Cowdall hall,* and commanded a great part of Wearyholme;† soe that, April 26, the Garrison began to grase their Cattell on the east side of the towne, near the Cittydell;‡ to beat them from

* Coldall-hall, see page 15, *note.*

† Weary-holme, now called Willow-holme, is near the junction of the Caldew and the Eden, on the west side of the former river, and about half a mile from the city.

‡ The citadel was situated at the south-east angle of the city, near the English-gate, and consisted of two immense cir-

which plaine, the roundheads raised a work at Fuis hill,§ yet the cattell continued to grase towards the Swift,‖ which moved the beseigers, to put all their horse, Scotch and English, in readinesse, and to give the Garrison but one blow; for the surprise of all their Cattell.

Captaine Robert Philipson (who succeeded in the place of Toppam) had the guard; and in the morning grassed all the Cattell as far as Bocherby

cular towers, one hundred and seventy feet apart from one another, but united by a strong curtain wall, on the inner side of which, pointing towards the market-place, was, besides some other buildings, a half-moon battery, commanding the principal street of the city. It was surrounded by a deep ditch.

Of the two towers, that on the west was strictly circular, but the eastern one was oval shaped; the latter, with new battlements and windows, and some few other alterations, remains at present, substantially the same as formerly; the western tower was razed to the ground, and entirely rebuilt on the same site, in its present form.

The citadel is said, originally, to have been erected by William Rufus, but being in a state of ruin and decay, it was re-edified in the sixteenth century, by Henry VIII., and was repaired and enlarged by subsequent monarchs. Some of the apartments in the citadel, such as the great hall, the buttery, and the boulting house, are particularly specified in the MS. account of its dilapidations and military stores, taken in the reign of Queen Elizabeth, and preserved in the British Museum, (Cott. MSS. Titus F. XIII. No. 29.)

In the year 1807, an act of parliament was obtained for the purpose of enabling "his majesty to grant the citadel and walls of the city of Carlisle, &c., to the justices of peace for the county of Cumberland, for building courts of justice for the said county," &c. Three years after the passing of the act, the alteration and rebuilding of the towers, to the extent already mentioned, and the construction of some additional buildings, was commenced under the direction of R. Smirke, jun., Esq., R.A., and they were so far completed as to be used for the assizes in the following year, (1810;) but their internal decorations were not finished till about ten years later.—*History of Carlisle.*

§ Between Botchergate and Botcherby Mill.

‖ A large meadow, east of the castle, having the Eden on its east and north sides.

mill. The beseiged, observing the barrakade at Stanwix to be taken away, gave the first suspicion to S[r] Thomas Glenham of some sudden designe; who p'sently commanded Philipson to draw neere the Towne wth the Cowes, and to be very diligent, which he did; and by y[t] means secured both the men and the Cowes. Towards noon, upon the unloading of their little Falcon, about 800 horse from Stanyix, S. Nicolas, Bocherby, [and] Rickerby, come powdering towards the Cowes so fast, that ere Philipson could get the Cowes driven, both he and they were engaged on every side; yet the guard desperately charged throug the enemie, and brought the cattell with them, wth the losse of 6 Cowes and 15 horses; when in all p'bability neither horse nor man could escape them. Philipson run one Kenity through the body, up to the hilts, who turning suddenly about, wrested his sword out of his hand, and went of to his quarters at Park brome,* with the sword in his body, boasting y[t] he had encountred and Disarmed little Philipson. Major Agnew, a Scot, was 3 times shot, but not mortally, Livetenant Scot was killed, and divers others slaine and hurt. The Cavalerers lost one Anderson, a trouper, and a poor old townsman, who was no souldier. A servant or two, who bore no arms, were hurt.

Aprill 29th a p'tie of the Garrisons horse vapouring towards Newlathes, killed 2 skouts; and brought away their horses.

May 1st Captaine Robert Philipson commanded the guard, who grased the cattell in Weary holme; and being alarm'd by the towling of the great bell, was pointed by the flagg to some of the enemies foot, who from a hedge, were fireing at the cattell: these he beat from the hedge, killed two, and dispersed the rest.

* Park-Broom is a hamlet, on the north bank of the Eden, about three miles north-east of Carlisle, in the township of Linstock and parish of Stanwix.

May 3^d the cattell grased in Denton holme,* from whome 6 horse went towards Newleaths, where they killed the skout; and riding further through Blackall wood, they espied a troupe of the enemies horse grasing, which they attempted to bring in; but being pursued by another troupe, were forced to quit them.

May 4th the elder Philipson commanded the Guard, who grased them in the same place, towards which 3 or 4 of the enemies horse vapoured; but p'sently, one of them being mortally shott with a fowling peice, they drew of towards noon. The enemies drew out some foot to a hedge, who were repulsed by Philipson, wth two of their deaths: but under a little hill he unexpectedly mett wth Major Cholmley, a pretty smart youth, comming towards him, in the head of his troupe. They charged each other furiously; Philipson ran through them with such violence, that some of them were unhorsed, and ere they could get into order, he charged them through the second time; soe routed them; and might have cut them all of, if Livetenant Ray, a blockhead, had come up wth the reserve to assist him, who was almost overpressed wth multitude. Thomas Wilson (alias Catcoats) was y^n shot through the foot by Cholmley; who, in requital, shot Chomley in the brest, but his arms secured him. The next morning, the Roundheads brought a number of countrey Labourers to raise a work on Morall hill,† who were soe cannonered from the Castle, y^t they run all away; yet afterwards they finished it. This day, Capt. Musgrave guarded the Cattell in ye Weary holme, and ye enimy offered twice or thrice to come downe; but, upon second thought, left the place.

On the 10 of May, Capt Philipson jun. grased in

* Denton-holme is on the west side of the city, on the other side of the Caldew.

† Near Shaddongate.

SIEGE OF CARLISLE.

the same place, who was troubled by some of the enemies Foot fireing upon them from Stanix Bank. Towards noon, Philipson and ye rest came, who sent a corporal with 20 horse, out of ye Scotch port, ordering the p'ty. to ride hastily over the bridge to Stanyix. At the lesser Bridge,* the skotts fired upon them [from] an outworke; but seeing the Cavallere come fiercely on, left their worke, and run into the towne. The Cavallere horse killed 5, took 2, and wounded 4 or 5; they took also 8 or 9 horses, and brought them wth the prisonners away, without any losse, but one horse shott, which was so fatt that he was sold for ten shillings a Quarter. If they had had any foot, they would have brought in their cannon. In the afternoon, the ever active Philipson rid out with 6 horse towards Legget hill,† and brought thence 11 of the Enemies horse grasing. Towards evening, the Roundheads horse came vapouring from Fuis hill, where Philipson met them, and with his musk. shot Livetenant Davison into the thighs, and his horse dead; the rest retreated.

May 11th Capt. Scisson had the guard, and grased in Weary holme. One Watson, poleing with a skott, was shot by his comraid; Scisson, to revenge his death, cut 2 of the Scotts, who fell downe [as] dead; but, as he was pursuing the rest, they rose up, and with much adoe recovered.

* Until of late years, there were two bridges over the Eden between Carlisle and Stanwix—the river dividing itself into two branches; the principal stream ran nearest to the city: and until the conclusion of the sixteenth century, two wooden structures, respectively called Eden and Prestbeck Bridges, formed the communication between Carlisle and Stanwix. In 1600, an act of parliament passed for rebuilding them of stone. 'The lesser bridge,' mentioned in the text, was therefore over that branch of the river which flowed nearest to Stanwix, and adjoining to the site of which the present bridge was erected in the years 1812—15, when the entire stream was diverted into one channel.

† Legget-hill is at the east end of the Swifts, and near the confluence of the Petterl with the Eden.

SIEGE OF CARLISLE.

May 13th. About supper time, the alarum bel tolled, upon the advance of all the enemies horse from every Quarter towards the Cattell, neere the Swift: whereupon Little Philipson, having got a sword, galloped to the Cavaleres, who were in no order, rallied y^m Quickly into rank and file, put the Roundheads to retreat, and fired at them a great way in the arrere. This done, Capt Lainam, a Cornish man, of an undaunted spirit, wth Andrew Knagg and two or three more, rid directly to the Scotch out work at Stanyix, and fetched from thence 3 horses. If any censure this brave and prudent pson. for exposing himself to soe many shots, for soe poor a booty, let them call to mind that of Tacitus: "*Nullum magnum ingenium sine aliquâ mixturâ dementiæ.*" The like example we had this Evening, in young Philipson, who not content to drive such numerous horse out of ye field, stay'd vapouring with a few of their Commanders, till he was dangerously shot in the back by a Boy, which made him useless during the seige. Hinks y^t night, being lame in that hand he was shot in, brought away two horses on the sands,* which Lanian had left, having above a hundred bullets shot at him from the work at Stanyix. This Evening, a letter of the King to Sr Thomas Glenham, was sent from Skipton, which was read the next day in ye Church; expressing his Maties purpose to releive Carlile, if they could hold out a while longer; and that for that end, he was marched as far as Chester.

May 15th. The horse was called in from grasing at Sermon time. Andrew Knagg, vapouring at fuis hill, was shot through the heart.

May 16th. The Roundheads begun a work at Swift hill,† to debarr the garrisons grasing on y^t side.

* An open space near the bridge over the Eden, where, in October, 1645, Sir John Brown, governor of Carlisle, defeated Lord Digby and Sir Marmaduke Langdale at the head of a small army.

† Swift hill; probably the eminence on the Swifts: see page 32.

In the morning, a 100 foot and 40 horse were commanded by Philipson to secure the Cattell grasing below that work; the foot were placed at a ditch nere Philipsons tower,* soe nigh the enemies work, y^t ye horsemen were compelled to sit on their horses, whilst they grased. The Enemie drew out some foot to peche against those in the ditch; but having one killed, drew of the rest. At nine in the morning, My Lord Kilkowbry† issued out with 300 horse from Stanyix, with resolution to break through the Musketeres at the Ditch; but was soe galled by their continual fireing, y^t he was forced to retreat; and Philipson wth his few horse charging their rere, the whole body came upon him soe fast, y^t he begun to make an easy orderly retreat, towards the Musketeres, wch he could not reach; wherefore he engaged wth them and routed them; two he killed in the pursuit, and Capt Rose. They carried away many led horses, but said they lost not their Riders. Of Capt Phillipsons p'ty, there were 4 hurt, but none slaine. The besiegers on ye walls could never see the Cavaleres p'tie after they closed, and were inclosed wth the Scots, but believed y^t the Scots were carrying them to Stanyix, when they grieved; at length they were chaising the Scots thither.

May 17th. a ptie. of Cavalere horse galloped after the Scots relief, who were going from a little worke at Catcoats bank; but before they could reach the houses, 4 or 5 were taken and killed.

On ye 19th Instant, Cholmley his men, wth the help of the countrey, raised a work not far from ye South port, which would have utterly deprived y^e

---

* This was probably one of the towers on the city walls.

† Robert Maclellan, Lord Kirkcudbright, knighted by James VI. of Scotland, to whom, and Charles I., he was gentleman of the Bedchamber, and by the latter created a Baron. He died without male issue, and the title descended to his nephew.

horses from grazing any longer. About 10 of the clok, when ye work was near finished, Capt Moore was commanded to issue out at the English port with 60 foot, who led his men Southwest of the work. Next after him, Capt. Dixon advanced wth 60 foot streight before ye work, and sheltered his men at a Ditch very near it. By this time ye horse drew out of the town in 5 pties.; one went towards St. Nicholas work, to hinder ye enemy from retreating to Chomlies great worke, in case they quit ye new one; all the rest marched ye high way towards it. After a little halt, began Moor, with a fast march, to advance towards ye south side of ye work: ye enemy fired brandly upon him, but hee returned them no answer, till he came within pistle shot. At the same time, from Chomlies mount, 100 foot advanced to assist ye little mount; while one of Dixons company threw in a fire ball, wch fell amongst their powder, and blew up spades, mattocks, and men. Soe y^t at once they leaped out of the work, and Mour entred it, haveing killed Conyers the Commander, who stoutly defended it. The first Division of the Cavaler horse met those in the face, who fled out of ye work, and had a Lamentable execution of them. Then they pursued the 100 foot afore mentioned to their very works; this Done, ye horse returned to the towne, and ye foot sent in 39 prisoners, where of diverse were pitifully burned by the granade. Then they levelled the work to the ground, and set the water in its right Course, wch the enemy had diverted, thereby to stop ye mills; and then returned with Six Dead men, 60 Muskets, &c., without the loss of any, save one Nesbut, shott through the head. In the afternoon they grased their Cattle where Troy once stood: I mean that bloody work. Major Cholmley sent for a list of the prisoners and had it.

May 20th Sr Thomas [Glenham] raised another worke, somewhat nearer the English port then that

SIEGE OF CARLISLE. 39

which he demolished yesterday; wch secured their meadowes to the Cattell.

May 23, the provision almost spent;[*] Mr. Skelton

[*] Previous to the commencement of the siege, the city was well victualled by the care of the gentry of the neighbourhood. The following were the contributions sent for the support of the garrison:—

	£	s.	d.
Sir Philip Musgrave, baronet	20	0	0
Sir Patricius Curwan, baronet	20	0	0
Sir Richard Graham, knight and baronet	20	0	0
Sir William Dalston, baronet, and Sir George Dalston	15	0	0
Sir Henry Fletcher, baronet	20	0	0
Sir John Lowther, baronet	20	0	0
Sir Edward Musgrave, baronet	10	0	0
Sir Edward Radcliffe, baronet	10	0	0
Sir Francis Howard, knight	10	0	0
Sir Charles Howard, knight	5	0	0
Sir Richard Sandford, knight	10	0	0
Sir Christopher Lowther, baronet, his son and heir	5	0	0
Sir William Musgrave, knight	5	0	0
Sir Timothy Fetherston, knight	5	0	0
Sir Thomas Dacre, knight	5	0	0
William Pennington esquire	10	0	0
Symon Musgrave esquire	2	0	0
William Carleton esquire	4	0	0
Leonard Dykes esquire	4	0	0
The earl of Anandale's estate	10	0	0
The lord Wharton's estate	10	0	0
Mr. Howard of Naward	20	0	0
John Dalston of Uldale esquire	5	0	0
William Lawson of Isell esquire	10	0	0
Mr. Salkeld of Whitehall	5	0	0
Mr. Lamplugh of Fells	4	0	0
Mr. Senhouse of Netherhall	2	0	0
Mr. Senhouse of Seascales	2	0	0
Mr. Barwise of Hildkirk	2	0	0
Mr. Salkeld of Brayton	2	0	0
Mr. Skelton of Armathwaite	5	0	0
Mr. Lamplugh of Dovenby	2	0	0
Mr. Blencoe of Blencoe	2	0	0
Mr. Fletcher of Moresby	5	0	0
Mr. Whelpdale of Penrith	5	0	0
Mr. Pennington of Seaton	4	0	0
Mr. Laton of Dailmain.	2	0	0

and Robt Feild were sent out to bring true Intelligence what hopes they might have of releif: who,

	£	s.	d.
Mr. Kirkbride of Ellerton	2	0	0
Mr. Fleming of Skirwith	2	0	0
Mr. Standley of Delegarth	2	0	0
Mrs. Hutton of Penrith	2	0	0
Mr. Patrickson of Paiswellhow	3	0	0
Mr. Richmond of Highet	2	0	0
Mr. Briscoe of Crofton	2	0	0
Mr. Denton of Cardew	2	0	0
Mr. Graham of Nunnery	2	0	0
Mr. Curwen of Camerton	2	0	0
Lady Curwen of Rottington	4	0	0
Mr. Warwick of Warwick brig	2	0	0
Mr. Tolson of Bridekirk	2	0	0
Mr. Fletcher of Tallentyre	2	0	0
Mr. Skelton of Branthwaite	2	0	0
Mr. Highmore of Armathwaite	2	0	0
Mr. Huddleston and his son of Hutton John	2	0	0
Mr. Irton of Irton	2	0	0
Mr. Latus of Millom	2	0	0
Mr. Harrington of Woolakes	4	0	0
Mrs. Fletcher of Calder Abbey	4	0	0
Mr. Dalston of Thwaites	2	0	0
Mr. Irton of Threlkeld	2	0	0
Mr. Swinburn of Lewthwaite and mother	2	0	0
Mr. Dalton of Brigham	3	0	0
Mr. Blennerhasset of Flemby	2	0	0
Mr. Joseph Porter	2	0	0
Mr. John Aglionby	2	0	0
Mr. Orfeur of Highclose	4	0	0
Mr. Brougham	2	0	0
Mr. Denton of Warnell	2	0	0
Mr. Dudley	2	0	0
Peter Winden of Lorton	1	0	0
Mr. Robert Fisher	1	0	0
Mr. Thomas Benson	1	0	0
Mr. Osmotherly of Langrigg	1	0	0
Mr. Chambers of Raby Coat	1	0	0
Mr. Salkeld of Threapland	1	0	0
Mr. Richard Eglesfield	1	0	0
Mr. Denton of Bothel	1	0	0
Mr. Dalston of Murkeholme	1	0	0
Mr. Anthony Bouch	2	0	0
Mr. Lathes	1	0	0
Mr. Ewan Christian of Unerigg	1	0	0

by a fire made at Barwick fields,† according to appointment, gave notice of their return and were secured by a party who brought them in.

	£	s.	d.
Mr. Wivell of Johnby	1	0	0
Mrs. Buckle of Lamonby	1	0	0
Mr. Henry Baxter	1	0	0
Mr. Miles Halton	1	0	0
Mr. Fielding	2	0	0
Mr. Threlkeld of Melmerby junior	1	0	0
Mr. John Pildrem	1	0	0
Mr. Lamplugh of Ribton	1	0	0
Edward Walker of Lasonby	1	0	0
Dr. Sybson for temporalities	1	0	0
Mr. William James	1	0	0
Mr. Barrow of Skelton	1	0	0
Mr. Clement Skelton	1	0	0

Clergymen:

	£	s.	d.
The dean and chapter of Carlisle, viz. the dean 4l., and every prebend 30s.	10	0	0
Mr. Usher of Kirk Andrews	3	0	0
Mr. Constable of Arthuret	3	0	0
Mr. Welchman of Stanwix	1	0	0
Mr. Head of Aikton	3	0	0
Mr. Warwick for Bowness and Brampton	2	0	0
Mr. Burton of Orton	2	0	0
Mr. Priestman for Kirklinton	1	0	0
Dr. Sibson for Bewcastle or the sequestrators	2	0	0
Mr. Gibson for Castle Carrick	1	0	0
Mr. Morland for Graystock	5	0	0
Mr. West for Addingham	1	0	0
The sequestrators of Great Salkeld parsonage	1	0	0
Mr. Goodwin of Lasonby	1	0	0
Mr. Sharpless of Croglin	1	0	0
Mr. Milburne for Skelton and Ouseby	2	0	0
Mr. Langbaine for Keswick	2	0	0
Mr. Tunstell for Caldbeck	2	0	0
Mr. Hudson for Uldale and Kirkbride	2	0	0
Mr. Robinson for Torpenhow	2	0	0
Mr. Fairfax for Bolton	2	0	0
Mr. Fletcher of Plumland	2	0	0
Mr. Wilkinson of Gilcrux	1	0	0
Mr. Beck of Brumfield	1	10	0
Mr. Cookson of Brigham	1	0	0
Mr. Fletcher of Dean	2	0	0
Mr. Lowther of Workington	2	0	0

May 26th. They delivered a letter to Sr Thomas Glenham, from Sr Richard Wallis,‡ governor of newark, who said he had expresse command from the king, to advertise them that he was come as farre as Latham house,§ with resolution to releive them, in convenient time. This evening Sr Alexander Hamilton, major generall of the Scotch horse, Sr John Broune,¶ Colonell, Livetenant Colonell Hogg, major Barwis, &c., sounded a parlie at the Irish bridge. Sr Thomas Glenham, wth other commanders, went out to them. The Scotts business was for a surrender; but the governurs would hear of nothing but sack: soe they parted merrily.

May 29th. The Cattel grased in Denton holm, about a Muskett shot beyond the enimies work at morall hill.** A countrie Capt., not to be known but by ye burning of his boote at one of the garrison's bonefires, disdaining that 25 horse should approach soe near his peacefull Quarters, drew downe in two bodies, each consisting of forty a peice,

		£	s.	d.
Mr. Antrobus of Egremond	..	.	1 10	0
Mr. Fletcher of Distington	..	..	1 10	0
Mr. Hudson of Harrington	..	..	2 0	0
Mr. Tubman of Whitcham	..	..	1 0	0
Mr. Braithwaite of Lamplugh	..	..	1 0	0

The sum total 463 10 0

† Barrock, in the parish of Hesket-in-the-Forest, about six miles south of Carlisle.

‡ Sir Richard Willis succeeded, in the governorship of Newark, Sir Richard Byron, who had been displaced by the king's commissioners.

§ Lathom-House in Lancashire, a seat of the Earl of Derby, is well-known on account of the gallant siege it sustained under the command of the celebrated Charlotte de la Tremouille, wife of James, seventh Earl of Derby, when attacked by the parliamentarians, in 1644, under Sir Thomas Fairfax.

¶ Sir John Brown, soon after the conclusion of the siege, was appointed governor of Carlisle. In October, 1645, he defeated a small army on Carlisle Sands, under the command of Lord Digby and Sir Marmaduke Langdale.

** Near Shaddongate, west of the city.

SIEGE OF CARLISLE. 43

soe eagerly as if he had not got his breakfast; but the   begun to charge, he faced about, haveing forgott his foot at home; y[e] party pursued him half a mile to Comersaile.* They killed 4 or 5, and brought away 3 prisoners; but *Turno tempus erit*,† they rested not long till he appeared in the head of the same horse, wth 100 foot, towards whom six of y[e] Cavaleres were sent out to discover his number; but he, scorning to contest wth six, face about againe; some say, as fast as if all the horse in the towne had been at his heels; and, to show how much he sleighted to take advantage of them, threw away his sword, w[ch] was taken up by one of the pursuers.

May 30th. Capt Blenkinshop came in with newes y[t] the king was come into Westermerland, and y[t] Leslie had warned y[e] Countries carts to fetch away his badgige; which caused the ioyfull garrison to eat that day Three days provision, and repent wth a cup of cold water for three dayes after. At this time three shillings peeces were coined out of the Cyttysens plate.‡

June the 1 and 3. Henry Sims, John Brotherick, and Edward Hind, died of former wounds.

June 5th. Major Backstorguld‖ ye Citty with a gross lye; y[t] the king had taken Manchester and would be with them p'sently; *facilè credimus quod volumus:* and no wonder, [considering] their small quantity of hors flesh without Bread or salt.

                                    hempseed, dogs, and rats were eaten, made them listen after releif.§ June 6th, therefore yet more were sent out to disabuse ye garrison, and to bring in certaine word whether was to be expected releife or surrender; these were Capt. Lanion, Capt. Moore, Mr. Norgate, Mr. Gilpin, and Robt Feild.

June 8th. Major Macdaggal and capt Bartram

---

* Cummersdale.   † Virgilii Æneidos, lib. x. 503.
‡ See note, page 13.   ‖ Deceived.
§ This sentence is incomplete in the MS.

were commanded with 200 Foot to assault the work at Stanniks; while Capt Phillipson, with some horse, ride a great way beyond Stanniks, to fetch in 37 Cowes and 19 horses, wch when they were come safe over y^e water, Philipson charged those in the towne, and y^e Commanders of y^e foot tooke their worke and three pece of small cannon in it, wth Cloaks, arms, and meal.

June 9$^{th.}$ Feild and ensine Orton came in with streight stories, but as grosse lies as any of the former, of the kings being in Yorkshire, and Smarmake langdailes* hastie martch towards them through Lankashire. Now were Gentlemen and others so shrunk that they could not chuse but laugh one at another to see their closet† hang as upon men on gibbets; for one might have put theire head and fists between the doublet and the shirts of many of them. The foot would be now and then stealing away, but not a man of ye Cavalere.

June ye 11th six troupers went wthout orders to Commersdale milne to fetch some corne; being a mile and a half from ye towne; they had a little re-

---

* Sir Marmaduke Langdale, knighted at Whitehall, by Charles I., 5th February, 1627, was the son and heir of Peter Langdale, Esq., of Pighill, near Beverley, co. York. In 1642, he was high-sheriff of that county; and in the following year, he had the command of the horse under the Earl of Newcastle, when he routed the Scots, at Corbridge, in Northumberland. He, with Sir Philip Musgrave, attended Charles II. during his exile, when he was advanced to the dignity of a baron of this kingdom, by the title of Baron Langdale. On the 9th October, 1660, he was constituted lord-lieutenant of the West Riding of the county of York, and of the city and county of York, and custos rotulorum thereof. He died in 1661, at Holme, in the East Riding, and was buried at Santon. See further particulars respecting Sir Marmaduke in the Historical Account prefixed to this Narrative. The title of Baron Langdale became extinct, in 1777, by the death of his great-great-grandson, without issue; but it was revived in 1836, in the person of Henry Bickersteth, now (1840) Master of the Rolls.

† Clothes.

serve. They brought away 14 bushells, and went again for more with 14 horse, all the other horse standing for a reserve at Denton holme. W^n the 14 horse were loaden and returning, a Regiment of horse, of my lord D.house,* advanced to Denton holme. After a small debate, the Cavaliers, overcharged wth numbers, were repulsed to the water side; but there they rallied, charged their first p'ty, and made them retreat. But ye whole body charging, the kebs were put to a second retreat, leaving Mackarty and Philipson with others engaged amongst them, who continually releiving one another, fought themselves free, and came to their p'ty wthout hurt, save a sleight cut which Philipson received in his face.

About this time, the horse y^t went for ye Corn, seeing such multitudes in their way, threw it all downe; and intending to wheel about into the towne, they fell amongst a company of foot, who fired [so] fiercely upon them, that they resolved to break through Dahowes† his regiment; who, supposing them to be of their own p'ty, enquired of them which was the best way to charge Philipson through the water. They answered, "this," and every man directing his pistoll at an enemies face, they charged through the whole body to Philipson, who encouraged by them and some other horse that came to him from the towne, gave them forthwith a third charge soe gallantly, y^t he forced ye whole

* Query. William Ramsay, first Earl of Dalhousie; so created by Charles I. *Ob.* 1674.

Lieutenant-General the Hon. J. Ramsay, son of the late Earl of Dalhousie, and a descendant from the above Earl, was the last governor of Carlisle. By his death, which occurred in 1837, the ancient office of governor of Carlisle,—which was of great consequence in the earlier periods of the history of this city,—became extinct, in accordance with a previous determination, that no appointment to that office should again be made.

† Lord Dalhousie.

regiment to run, killed 13, [and] wounded many, (Major Bickerton for one, who was shot through his heel,) brought in Coronell, and another prisoner, wth 6 of their dead men. What could [not] these worthies have atchieved, if they had not co in a pinfold and pined with hunger? This night, Robt Feild came in, who brought them a p'cell of half newes, by order of them (as was supposed) who thought it good pollicie to make lies their refuge. But they could p'vaile noe longer: hunger was so extreame, y^t it could scarce be concealed from the enemies. Philipson therefore was sent to York, with an English and Scots parliament Capt. to know my Lord Fairfax and generall Leslyes pleasure; whether ye surrendered to ye English or Scotch: about which [the] generall sideing with his party, offered any conditions, to them who could not have lived 10 days after they articled with them.

June 17 they received another lym expressing y^t the kings Forces, under prince Maurice,[*] had taken Glocester by storm; y^t ye king himselfe had taken Leicester, Derby, and Chesterfield, with all the enemies bagg and baggage; and was marching day and night to the releife of Carlile. Whereas the only truth was, y^t the king had taken Leicester; wch was a bate laid in his way, till they were ready to give England y^r fatal Blow at Naseby,[†] wch the garrison understood not, till they heard the cannon and great vollies of musketts from ye besciegers works. This afternoon, divers officers came with soldiers into the common Backouse,[‡] and took away all the hors flesh from ye poor people, who were as neere starving as themselves. The beseigers perceiving the Cavaliers, who were scarce able to walk in the streets, not to issue out as they were wont, grew insolent, and vapoured amane.

[*] Brother of Prince Rupert.
[†] The battle of Naseby, which proved so fatal to the prospects of Charles I., was fought on the 14th of June, 1645.
[‡] Bakehouse.

June 20. one died in ye towne, who, wereing a blue cap wch he had taken from ye Scotch at Stannix, was mistaken in ye last action at Denton holme, received his death wound by Richard grave, a Cavalier.

June 22. Sr Thomas Glenham received a Letter from Leslie adviseing him not to treat wth English, who lay before them, whom he called—Sirs, and something else, and such has had neither courage nor power to ptect.* him after surrender, and that on the contrary from him they should have their own tearmes and security. Y^e governor, who could not deny ye antecedent, granted ye consequent. Y^e garrison had now but half a pound of hors flesh for 4 dayes.

June 23. The towns men humbly petitioned Sr Thos Glenham y^t their horse flesh might not be taken from them as formerly; and informed him y^t they were not able to endure ye famine any longer; to wch he gave no answer, nor redresse, in 4 dayes space; at which time, a few woomen of ye scolds and scum of the citty, mett at ye cross, braling against Sr Henry Stradling there p'sent; who first threatned to fire upon them; and when they replyed they [would] take it as a favor, he left them wth tears in his eyes, but could not mend their Commons. Dr Burwell was ye only man who to this time had pserved. a little Barrel of strong ale, unknowne to any but Sr Tho Glenham. Y^e first commander sent to treat with Sr Tho., was made so drunk wth this ale, that, at his return to Lesly, he could give him no account of his errand, nor utter a wise word.

The next day Lesly [sent] in a graver person; who, being assured by Sr Tho: y^t the towne should be surrendered, offered to take his leave with great satisfaction; but was, in civility, conducted by him

---

* Protect.

to ye Scots ports,* where ye corporall being ordered not to appeare, soe y^t the Scott could not presently passe, Sr Tho. intreated him to take a short repose In the next house, wch was Chanceller Burrels quarter; where, calling for his ale, the Cavalleres drunk water, and ye Scot ale soe excessively, y^t he returned to Leslie In ye same pickle wth ye former, professing y^t ye Garrison was every where full of strong drink.

But the next day, being 25th of June, the Articles were agreed upon, and ye citty of Carlyle, little in circuite, but great and memorable for Loyalty, received a Scots garrison upon the 28. of June, upon these noble articles, wch by David Lesleys strict command and p'sonall conduct were punctually performed, both to those y^t marched out, and to the Cittysons y^t staid at Home.

FINIS.

Desiderantur Articuli.†

* The north or Scotch gate.
† The Articles, which are omitted in the British Museum copy, are supplied in the Historical Account prefixed to this publication.